e EYFS:

etting it right?

oni and Sue Bristow

Featherstone

First published 2010 by A&C Black Publishers Limited
This edition published 2013 by Featherstone, an imprint of Bloomsbury Publishing plc
50 Bedford Square
London
WC1B 3DP
www.bloomsbury.com

ISBN 978-1-4081-8682-4

Text © Anita Soni and Sue Bristow
Design © Bob Vickers

A CIP record for this publication is available from the British Library.

Printed by CPI Group (UK) Ltd, Croydon, CR0 4YY

10 9 8 7 6 5 4 3 2 1

This book is produced using paper that is made from wood grown in
managed, sustainable forests. It is natural, renewable and recyclable.
The logging and manufacturing processes conform to the environmental
regulations of the country of origin.

To see our full range of titles
visit www.bloomsbury.com

Contents

Introduction and rationale

Who is this book for?

This book has been written for early years practitioners who work with children from birth to the end of the academic year in which the children are five years old. This includes those practitioners working in maintained and independent schools, in private and voluntary sector settings and childminders.

How does it relate to the reformed Early Years Foundation Stage (EYFS)?

The Early Years Foundation Stage (EYFS) was first implemented in all settings in England in 2008. The reformed EYFS was published in March 2012. Practitioners, managers, parents and children need to know how successful the implementation of the EYFS has been, and what still needs to be done. The original EYFS (DCSF 2008) and the reformed EYFS (DfE, 2012/Early Education, 2012/ Foundation Years, 2012) contains a lot of information in different formats, and this can appear daunting. This book aims to help practitioners and leaders to break up the EYFS into manageable, bite-sized chunks. It provides a simple, user-friendly way of evaluating practice against the EYFS, and assists in the long-term and short-term planning for development in key areas.

Why is self-evaluation important?

The book contains a framework that will enable practitioners to self-evaluate their practice and provision against the EYFS, and celebrate successes and identify priorities for improvement. This book provides the raw materials for a setting to consistently and continuously improve the standards of practice. The Effective Provision of Pre-School Education Project (EPPE, 2003) found that higher quality provision helps children to make a good start in life. The Early Years Quality Improvement Support Programme (EYQISP, National Strategies 2008) cited on the Foundation Years website states:

> 'Quality is the key to securing improved outcomes for children and giving them a better start in the early years.'

Self-evaluation is an important part of professional development and should be undertaken regularly in all settings. The EYQISP also encourages:

> 'a continuous cycle of self evaluation, improvement and reflection, thus empowering practitioners to see themselves as learners, seeking improvements in their practice...'

Whilst it is no longer compulsory to complete the self-evaluation form supplied by OfSTED, it is strongly recommended, and;

> '...inspectors will still check to see what self-evaluation you carry out and make a judgement about how effective this is.' (OfSTED, 2011)

Self-evaluation enables you as practitioners to look at your own development and the development of your setting, not just relying on the views and opinions of inspectors and advisers, who may not have the deep knowledge of the context of your situation. This should help reassure those working at the setting that they are implementing the EYFS. This reassurance should lead to greater confidence when speaking to inspectors and advisers, as you will be able to explain why things are the way they are at your setting. It will also provide you with key information as you plan for development of the staff within your setting and prepare for inspections and discussions with your local authority staff team.

This book offers evaluation audits that will involve you and the parents (if you wish) in:

- reflecting on your own practice and how well you know your key children;
- considering the resources and experiences you provide for children;
- examining your indoor and outdoor environment;
- reflecting on the requirements within the reformed Statutory Framework, the Commitment cards of the EYFS, the Characteristics of Effective Learning and the seven areas of Learning and Development in the *Development Matters in the EYFS*;
- celebrating success and planning for improvement.

What do I need for the evaluation?

There are a number of questionnaires and tools within the book which can be used for your self-evaluation audit:

1. Questions to support reflection on the reformed *Statutory Framework*;

2. 2 Principles into Practice questionnaires for parents and practitioners to identify a commitment to celebrate and a commitment to work on;

3. 15 Commitment card questionnaires, one for each of the 15 Commitment cards (4.4 Areas of Learning and Development is incorporated in the Areas of Learning and Development questionnaire);

4. A sample evidence collection sheet;

5. 3 Characteristics of Effective Learning questionnaires for practitioners

6. Areas of Learning and Development questionnaires for parents and practitioners to identify the areas to celebrate and those to work on;

7. Practitioner questionnaires for three age bands (0–20 months, 16–36 months, 30–60+ months) for each of the seven areas of Learning and Development. These examine the practice of the adults, knowledge of the uniqueness of the children and the environment.

Who should be involved in the evaluation?

Everyone in your setting should be involved in regular review and evaluation – practitioners, other employees, parents (although the term 'parent' is used within this book this applies to the main carers of the child while at your setting) and the children themselves. If all practitioners (full and part-time) are involved in the process, this will affect the pace and timescale of the process but in the long term makes it more effective. This book is intended for use with practitioners and parents, but views from other regular visitors such as the speech and language therapist, health visitors, and support advisers will make the information richer and more effective.

You may want to select or adapt parts of the questionnaires for some parents, and this helps to make the process your own. We have included parent versions of the Principles into Practice questionnaire and Areas of Learning and Development questionnaire as possible versions but you may need to adapt them to suit the parents at your setting. Remember to think about the languages your parents speak and the type of words they use; this will help you to adapt the questionnaires as required.

When should I use the questionnaires?

You can choose to use the questionnaires in supervision sessions with staff as the reformed Statutory Framework has stated:

> 'Providers must put appropriate arrangements in place for the supervision of staff who have contact with children and families. Effective supervision provides support, coaching and training for the practitioner and promotes the interests of children. Supervision should foster a culture of mutual support, teamwork and continuous improvement...'

You may want to work with the whole staff team, or staff who work with one age group and have identified areas to work on, or a single staff member to support their practice as part of the 'coaching to improve their personal effectiveness'. (DfE, 2012)

How long will the process of evaluation take and how should it be managed?

All evaluation takes time, and this version is no exception. You can undergo the process in small sections over the course of a year, or in bigger chunks in a shorter period. If the evaluation is going to be successful, you need to allow time as you go through each stage in turn, in order that you can:

- collect information, opinions and observations;
- collate and consider these;
- decide what the information is telling you;
- identify strengths and needs;
- plan to celebrate the successes and address the needs you have identified.

You could manage this process through:

- a series of staff meetings;
- whole staff development days.

It is important to identify a person or a couple of people to coordinate the process, as they will be responsible for keeping to an agreed timetable for each of the stages above – but it is also important to involve everyone!

How you undertake the process at your setting is up to you, but it is worth deciding when you are going to start the evaluation, and giving all staff notice of what is going to happen. 'How do I use this book?' (see page 7) gives more detailed guidance on our suggested approach, and in 'Getting started' (see page 9) there are examples of how some settings may choose to use the book, dependent on their circumstances. However, you may have strong ideas about what you want to focus on and can use the questionnaires and evidence sheets in this book flexibly to support the development of your setting.

Final messages...

Children are unique and will vary within each age band. The age bands on the questionnaires are broad and are to be used flexibly. There is considerable development from the beginning to the end of each age band. In this book, the age bands of the EYFS have been combined from six overlapping age bands to three overlapping age bands to make it manageable for settings and practitioners.

A final point is not to be daunted by the number of questionnaires! You are not supposed to do them all in one go. Take it stage by stage and use the questionnaires as adaptable tools to use in the way that suits you, the setting, the children and the parents.

How do I use this book?

There are four stages to the book:

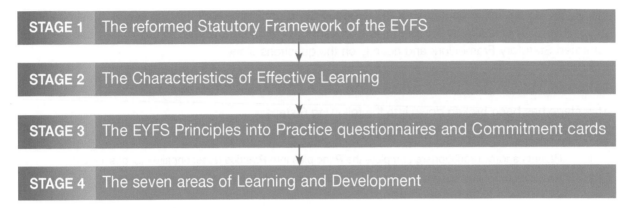

STAGE 1	The reformed Statutory Framework of the EYFS
STAGE 2	The Characteristics of Effective Learning
STAGE 3	The EYFS Principles into Practice questionnaires and Commitment cards
STAGE 4	The seven areas of Learning and Development

Within each stage the same process will be followed as recommended in the EYQISP (National Strategies, 2008).

- Reflect (self-evaluation audit – collect the evidence)
- Rate (identify and agree improvement priorities)
- Celebrate success
- Prioritise areas for development (focused improvement plan)
- Actions
- Collect evidence and celebrate (review)

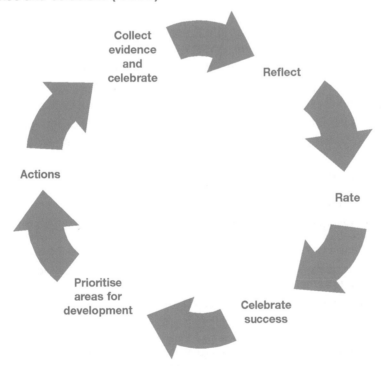

You can use this simple, step-by-step approach suggested. Alternatively, you may want to evaluate a specific commitment or area of Learning and Development that you know needs work on. If this is the case you may choose to focus on a certain section of the book. It is up to you to decide what is appropriate for your setting. In writing this book we recognise that just as every child is unique, so is every setting.

The self-evaluation process

Stage 1 Evaluation based on the Statutory Framework of the EYFS (Dfe, 2012)

Initially review the implementation of the reformed Statutory Framework through use of questions on pages 14–16. This is a legal framework and so cannot be worked towards, so it is vital to use the reformed Statutory Framework and not rely on the questions alone.

Stage 2 The EYFS Principles into Practice questionnaires and Commitment cards

This stage has been broken down into the following 6 steps:

Step	
1	Parents and/or practitioners complete the Principles into Practice questionnaires (pages 19–21).
2	Analyse completed questionnaires and identify one successfully implemented commitment and one commitment to further develop.
3	Celebrate the successfully completed commitment through development of a display or book on that Commitment card.
4	Reflect on the Commitment card that requires further development by completing the relevant Commitment card questionnaire, looking at areas where more work is needed or to enhance what is going on (pages 25–39).
5	Complete an action plan (page 40) based on the questionnaires and work through the actions. Collect evidence to show what has been implemented. Use this evidence to make a display or book to demonstrate to yourself, children, parents and Ofsted that your planned actions have been successfully completed.
6	Repeat steps 4 and 5 with another commitment that needed development.

Stage 3 The Characteristics of Effective Learning

This stage has been put in after the Principles into Practice Commitment cards as it has been emphasised in the *Development Matters in the EYFS* (Early Education, 2012). The three Characteristics of Effective Learning are interconnected with the three prime and four specific areas of learning and development. There are three questionnaires that can be used with all practitioners to evaluate understanding of: Play and Exploring, Active Learning and Creativity and Critical thinking. The three questionnaires take a similar format to those for the areas of Learning and Development in that they evaluate practitioners' knowledge of their key children, their practice and the environment.

Stages 4 The seven areas of Learning and Development

This stage has been broken into the following 6 steps:

Step	
1	Parents and/or practitioners complete the Areas of Learning and Development questionnaires.
2	Analyse completed questionnaires and identify one area of Learning and Development that can be celebrated and one to further develop.
3	Celebrate the success in an area of Learning and Development by creating an information book or display on that area of learning and development.
4	Reflect on the area of Learning and Development that requires further work. This can be done by practitioners completing the relevant questionnaires for that area, looking at where more knowledge of key children, development of practice or the environment is needed or to enhance what is going on.
5	Complete an action plan based on the questionnaires and work through the actions. Collect evidence to show what has been implemented. Use this evidence to make a display or book to demonstrate to yourself, children, parents and Ofsted that your planned actions have been successfully completed.
6	Repeat steps 4 and 5 with a different area of Learning and Development.

Getting started

The following examples show how various settings have adopted this self-evaluation approach.

Setting A   Nursery and Reception Unit within a school

Ofsted judged them 'satisfactory' with several areas identified. The team are developing their action plan and need to identify a timeline with which to achieve the actions. There is disagreement within the team about which action to start with.

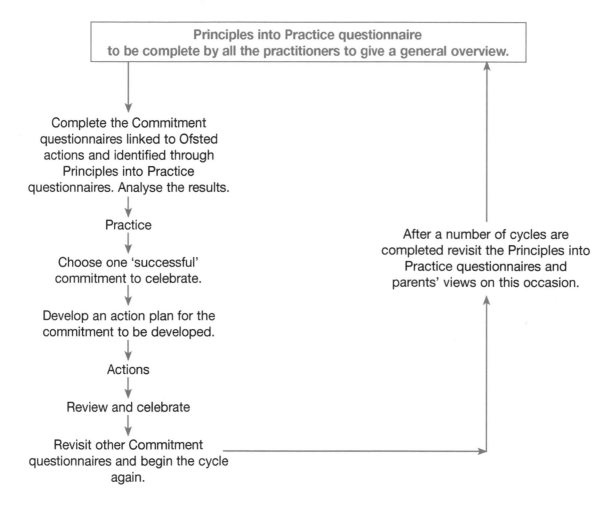

Setting B Playgroup

OFSTED judged it 'inadequate'.

> **Principles into Practice questionnaire**
> to be complete by all the practitioners and parents to give a general overview.

Complete the Commitment
questionnaires linked to Ofsted
actions and identified through
the Principles into Practice
questionnaires. Analyse the results.

Choose one 'successful' commitment to celebrate

Develop an action plan for the commitment to be developed.

Actions

Review and celebrate

Revisit other Commitment
questionnaires and begin the cycle again.

> **After a number of cycles have been completed revisit the Principles into Practice questionnaires. When ready, move onto the Areas of Learning and Development questionnaire.**

> **Areas of Learning and Development questionnaire**
> to be completed by all practitioners and parents to give a general overview.

The areas with the highest scores were:
CD all stages of development
PSED 30–60+ months
UW 0–20 and 16–36 months
Displays developed to celebrate the good practice within the nursery

The areas with the lowest score were:
PSED 0–20 months
CL 30–60+ months
MD 30–60+ months
PD 0–20 and 16–36 months

Action plan developed for PD 0–20 and 16–36 months and MD 30–60+ months

Actions

Review and celebrate

Revisit other areas of Learning and Development identified in first audit and complete cycle again.

> **After a number of cycles revisit the Areas of Learning and Development questionnaires again to work on the areas with the lowest scores.**

Setting C Nursery

Ofsted judged it 'good' in all areas with a key issue regarding their key person approach. In addition there has been a change in practitioners within the toddler room and two parents have expressed concern about how unsettled their children have become.

This setting has an identified need and focus of key person and therefore does not need the Principles into Practice questionnaires and Areas of Learning and Development questionnaires to prioritise need. If this setting chooses, it could use the 2.4 Key Person questionnaire alone with staff and parents to create an action plan to meet this identified need.

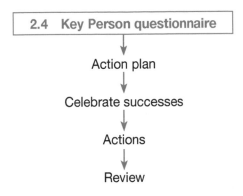

2.4   Key Person questionnaire

↓

Action plan

↓

Celebrate successes

↓

Actions

↓

Review

Setting D Childminder

Judged 'outstanding' in all areas by Ofsted. Six months after the inspection the childminder employed an assistant to work with her who was not confident working with the seven areas of Learning and Development as most of her experience has been with children aged under three.

Areas of Learning and Development questionnaire
filled out by practitioners.

↓

The areas with the highest scores were celebrated with a book of photos
and captions for parents and children to look at and to provide evidence
for external agencies.

↓

The areas with the lowest scores were analysed and prioritised.
An action plan was developed.

↓

Actions

↓

Review and celebrate

↓

Other areas of Learning and Development identified in the first audit were revisited
and the cycle was completed again.

↓

After a number of cycles, revisit the Areas of Learning and Development questionnaires
to work on the areas with the lowest scores.

Collecting evidence

It is important to have evidence to show what you have done and are doing. However, evidence can come in many forms, not just paper and it is important to remember this at all times.

What is evidence?

Evidence can be:

- Displays on the wall;
- Your planning;
- Comments, notes and cards from parents;
- How you interact and behave with the children;
- Children's comments;
- Photographs of the children, environment;
- Learning and development records or journals;
- Questionnaires by staff, parents or visitors;
- Visit notes from outside agencies such as local authority development officers, speech and language therapists, college placement supervisors and so on;
- Documentation such as policies and procedures;
- Reflections on your own practice;
- Observations;
- Children's work;
- Peer observations;
- Notes from staff meetings;
- Evaluations of planning;
- Maps of the environment;
- Action plans.

The EYFS: Am I getting it right? © Anita Soni & Sue Bristow

STAGE 1

The reformed Statutory Framework of the EYFS (Dfe, 2012)

This is the best place to start to have a quick check to ensure you are meeting the statutory requirements of the EYFS, before moving on to the rest of the book and further evaluating the quality at your setting.

The EYFS is given legal force through an Order and Regulations made under the Childcare Act 2006. It is mandatory for all schools and early years providers in Ofsted registered settings attended by young children – children from birth to the end of the academic year in which a child has their fifth birthday.

The EYFS (DfE, 2012) sets out:

● the learning and development requirements

● the safeguarding and welfare requirements.

The learning and development requirements are given legal force by the EYFS Order 2007 made under Section 39 (1) (a) of the Childcare Act 2006. The safeguarding and welfare requirements are given legal force by Regulations made under Section 39 (1) (b) of the Childcare Act 2006. The requirements have statutory force by virtue of Section 44 (1) of the Childcare Act 2006.

In order to help consider the legal requirements of the statutory framework, these have been listed, alongside some prompt questions. These can be used within staff meetings, as points of discussion to support staff in understanding the Statutory Framework for the EYFS. **However it is important to read the full Statutory Framework for the EYFS for guidance, detail and clarification on all points.**

The EYFS learning and development requirements with questions to prompt discussion and reflection:

Learning and Development requirements	Questions to support
The Early Learning Goals (ELGs) – This is the knowledge, skills and understanding which young children should have acquired by the end of the academic year in which they reach five. The Early Learning Goals establish the expectations for most children to reach by the end of the EYFS.	How do you plan and organise your setting to support the children in your setting achieving the Early Learning Goals by the end of their Reception year? How do you use the Early Learning Goals and Development Matters statements to inform and support your observation of and planning for the children in the setting? See the Statutory Framework for the EYFS (DfE, 2012) for full details on the Early Learning Goals.
The educational programmes for the seven areas of Learning and Development – The children must be provided with opportunities, experiences, encouragement and support to develop in the seven areas of Learning and Development.	Do staff know the seven areas of Learning and Development and what is within them? Which are the Prime areas of Learning and Development? Which are the four Specific areas of Learning and Development? Do you consider the educational programmes for the seven areas of Learning and Development when planning opportunities for the children in the setting? Do staff working with the youngest children (those aged under 3) focus strongly on the Three Prime areas of Learning and Development? How do you incorporate the individual needs, interests and stage of development of each child you care for to plan challenging but enjoyable experiences for the children in each area of Learning and Development? How do you provide opportunities for children who speak English as an Additional Language (EAL) to develop and use their home language? How do you provide an appropriate balance between activities led and guided by adults and those led by children? In planning how do you ensure children get opportunities to play and explore and actively learn? How do you encourage children to concentrate and persist when they encounter difficulties? In planning how do you encourage children to develop their own ideas, make links between ideas and develop their own strategies? Does every child and parent know who their key person is? How do parents understand the key person role? How are training and development needs of all staff members met in this setting? See the Statutory Framework for the EYFS (DfE, 2012) for full details on the educational programmes and the areas of learning and development.
Assessment – This plays an important part in helping parents, carers and practitioners to recognise children's progress, understand their needs and to plan activities and support.	When do you observe the children and respond to them appropriately to help them make progress? Are the learning experiences based on what practitioners observe in the children? Are your assessments based on your observations of what you see and hear children achieving and interested in? How are parents/carers kept up-to-date with their child's progress and development? How do practitioners address children's learning and development needs with parents and other relevant professionals? Is paperwork linked to assessment manageable and not require prolonged breaks from interacting with children? Is there a progress check completed on all children aged 2 and 3 years old? Is the EYFS Profile completed for all children in their final term of the year (Reception) in which they turn five? How are these assessments shared with parents? Do these written summaries reflect the development levels and needs of the individual child including areas of strength, and areas where additional support is needed? Are targeted support plans developed (identifying activities and strategies) for specific children to meet any significant emerging concerns or identified special educational need or disability? See the Statutory Framework for the EYFS (DfE, 2012) for full details on assessment.

The EYFS safeguarding and welfare requirements alongside questions to prompt discussion and reflection:

Welfare requirements	Questions to support
Child protection – Providers must be alert to any issues for concern in a child's life at home or elsewhere	Do you have an effective safeguarding policy and procedures in the setting? Do staff understand them and have current knowledge of safeguarding issues and procedures of the Local Safeguarding Children Board (LSCB)?
	Is there a designated person to lead responsibility for safeguarding in the setting who has attended relevant safeguarding training? Do all staff know who this is?
	Do all staff know how to identify signs of possible abuse and neglect and know how to respond?
	See the Statutory Framework for the EYFS (DfE, 2012) for full details on child protection.
Suitable people – Providers must ensure that people looking after children are suitable to fulfil the requirements of their role. The daily experience of children and overall quality of the provision depends on all practitioners having appropriate qualifications, skills, training and knowledge and a clear understanding of their roles and responsibilities. Staffing arrangements must meet the needs of all children and ensure their safety.	Do all staff who work directly with children, and other relevant adults aged over 16, have an enhanced criminal record disclosure?
	Are there systems in place to ensure people working with children, or have regular contact with them, are suitable?
	Are all staff aware what they have to disclose that may affect their suitability to work with children, both prior and during employment at the setting?
	Is all relevant information on staff (qualifications, identity checks, vetting processes, criminal record disclosures with dates and reference numbers) recorded?
	Are all providers aware of what would lead to disqualification, and how and when to notify Ofsted?
	Are providers aware of how to manage issues relating to staff taking medication and other substances?
	Are all new staff given induction training (including emergency evacuation procedures, safeguarding, child protection, equality policy and health and safety issues) to help them understand their roles and responsibilities?
	Are supervision arrangements in place for all staff who have contact with children and families to discuss issues, identify possible solutions and to improve their effectiveness?
	Do staff, including managers and deputies, in the settings have the appropriate qualifications?
	Are regular staff appraisals carried out?
	Are there continuous professional development opportunities including improvement of qualification levels available for staff?
	Are sufficient staff suitably trained in paediatric first aid?
	Has each child got an assigned key person?
	Are the minimum adult-child ratios met as defined in the Statutory Framework for the EYFS?
	See the Statutory Framework for the EYFS (DfE, 2012) for full details on suitable people, disqualification, staff taking medication or other substances, staff qualification, training support and skills, key person and staff : child ratios.
Health – Providers must promote the good health of children attending the setting.	Is there a procedure for responding to children who are ill or infectious? Is there a policy and procedure for administering medicines? How are these shared with parents?
	How do staff ensure they know the special health or dietary requirements, preferences and allergies that any child has? Is fresh drinking water available and accessible at all times?
	Is there an area that is suitable for hygienic preparation of food and drinks for babies and children? Do all staff hold the relevant qualification if involved in preparing and handling food?
	Is there a first aid box with appropriate contents accessible for use with children? Are written records of accidents, injuries and treatments kept?
	Are providers aware when and how to notify Ofsted of relevant incidents with regards to children's health?
	Is there a behaviour management policy a named practitioner for behaviour management who has the relevant skills?
	See the Statutory Framework for the EYFS (DfE, 2012) for full details on health including medicines, food and drink, accident or injury and managing behaviour.

The EYFS safeguarding and welfare requirements alongside questions to prompt discussion and reflection (continued):

Welfare requirements	Questions to support
Safety and suitability of premises, environment and equipment – Providers must ensure that premises including outdoor spaces are fit for purpose and clean. Spaces, furniture, equipment and toys must be safe for children to use and equipment must be clean and secure.	Is there a health and safety policy and procedures which cover identifying, reporting and dealing with accidents, hazards and faulty equipment? Are reasonable steps taken to ensure the safety of children in the case of a fire or other emergencies? Are the premises and equipment organised in a way that meets the needs of children, including sufficient space available as detailed in the Statutory Framework for the EYFS and to meet the needs of disabled children? Is access to outdoor play and activities provided on a daily basis (except in unsafe weather conditions)? Is there space for children who wish to relax, play quietly or sleep? Are there sufficient toilets and handbasins and hygienic changing facilities? Is there space for staff to talk to parents confidentially? Is there space for staff to take breaks away from areas used by children? Is the premises secure from unauthorised persons entering and are visitors' identities checked? Is there a clear and well-understood policy on risk assessment and are risk assessments reviewed regularly? Is parental consent gained for outings and how are children kept safe on them? See the Statutory Framework for the EYFS (DfE, 2012) for full details on safety and suitability of premises, environment and equipment including safety, smoking, premises, risk assessments and outings
Information and records – Providers must maintain records and obtain and share information appropriately to ensure the safe and efficient management of the setting and ensure the needs of all children are met.	Is there an equal opportunities policy and procedures that includes explanation of support for children with special educational needs and disability? How is a two way flow of information with parents/carers (and between providers if the child attends more than one setting) achieved? How are parents' comments included in children's records? Are parents/carers given appropriate access to all records on their child? Are records easily accessible and available? Is confidential information held securely? Is the appropriate, up-to-date information held on each child? Is accurate information, as indicated in the Statutory Framework for the EYFS, made available to parents? Is there a written procedure for complaints from parents/carers? Is the appropriate information held by the provider as indicated in the Statutory Framework for the EYFS? Are providers aware when and how to notify Ofsted of relevant changes? See the Statutory Framework for the EYFS (DfE, 2012) for full details on information and records, equal opportunities, information about the child, information for parents, complaints, information about the providers and changes that must be notified to Ofsted.

It is important that the setting meets these legal requirements (LA Advisors will be able to advise and support on this if needed). Once you have considered these questions; you are ready to move on to the next step, **Stage 2 The Principles into Practice questionnaire.**

STAGE 2

The Principles into Practice questionnaires and Commitment cards

The Principles into Practice Commitment cards form the basis of the EYFS and this is, therefore, the place to move on to after considering the *Statutory Framework*. The principles and commitments need to be implemented consistently to promote effective practice and quality within your setting. For your self-evaluation use the step-by-step approach outlined below.

STEP 1   Staff and parents to complete the Principles into Practice questionnaire.

There are two versions of the Principles into Practice questionnaire:

● one presents each commitment as a statement and then phrased as a question (for staff, see pages 19–20).

● one presents each commitment as a question (for parents, see page 21).

It is up to you which version you choose to use and photocopy. Choose the one that best suits the staff and parents at your setting.

Photocopy one questionnaire per staff member/parent. Ask each staff member and parent to rank how well they feel the setting is doing on each commitment by using a simple scale below:

1	2	3	4	5
Just starting work on this commitment				Fully implementing this commitment

When self-evaluating it is important to emphasise that high marks are not the order of the day but that it is important that everyone is honest about the practice in the setting and is willing and open to reflect on change. It is easier to complete this questionnaire quickly and not spend too long on considering each commitment in great depth as this is meant as a quick overview, and there is opportunity for detailed discussion later.

Compile the questionnaire results in the table on page 22. Write the scores (1, 2, 3, 4, 5) in the third and fourth columns for each person who has completed the questionnaire and then total them in the final column of the table.

Card number	Commitment	Scores		Total
		Practitioner's	Parent's	
1.1	Child Development			
1.2	Inclusive Practice			
1.3	Keeping Safe			
1.4	Health and Well-being			
2.1	Respecting Each Other			
2.2	Parents as Partners			
2.3	Supporting Learning			
2.4	Key Person			
3.1	Observation, Assessment and Planning			
3.2	Supporting Every Child			
3.3	The Learning Environment			
3.4	The Wider Context			
4.1	Play and Exploration			
4.2	Active Learning			
4.3	Creativity and Critical Thinking			

STEP 2 Analyse the completed questionnaires and identify a successfully implemented commitment and a commitment to develop.

Look carefully at the results of your completed questionnaires. The commitments with the highest scores are those that everyone feels the setting is doing very well, those with lower scores are the ones which would benefit from further development.

To develop practice further it is important to answer the questions honestly and to be able to prove which areas of the commitment are being already covered by filling in the evidence sheet (see page 24). The collated evidence sheets from all the staff will show the effective practice in place already and where the evidence is available but will also indicate where the evidence is required.

For example, for the question 'How do you support children's transitions between key person relationships in the setting when there are staff changes?' Possible evidence might be:
● the new key person visits the child in the room;
● parents are invited in to be introduced to the new key person and to visit the new room;
● a transition form on the child is filled in and passed on;
● the child visits the new key person and room.

Lack of evidence for the question will require staff to discuss this further and agree any actions that need to take place. See page 23 for an example of a completed evidence sheet.

STEP 3 Celebrate the successfully completed commitment.

Choose the highest scoring commitment. This is one that the setting is doing well, and celebrate! Make a display or book to demonstrate to yourself, children, parents and Ofsted that you are already doing this part of the EYFS well. The display or book should contain a variety of evidence including photographs, comments from parents and children, planning and children's work. This is important! It might be tempting to overlook those commitments that the setting is implementing successfully, but celebrating good practice is vital for the morale of staff, parents and children.

STEP 4 Reflect on the commitment to develop further by completing the appropriate Commitment card questionnaire.

Choose the commitment that scores the lowest, this is the commitment that requires some attention. Reflect on this commitment by asking everyone to complete a copy of the appropriate photocopiable Commitment questionnaire (see pages 25–39). The completed questionnaires and evidence sheets will show which parts of this commitment the setting needs to develop further.

STEP 5 Begin to act upon the Commitment questionnaire, develop practice further and collect evidence to show this is being implemented.

Analyse the responses to the questionnaires, and use this information to develop your practice. A photocopiable Action plan can be found on page 40. Collect evidence to show that the resulting actions taken have been successful. Use this evidence to make a display or book to demonstrate to yourself, the children, parents and Ofsted that your planned actions have been successfully completed. Ideas for development of practice can come from a number of sources including discussion and reflection with other practitioners and the relevant Principles into Practice Commitment card.

STEP 6 Repeat the relevant steps with a different, successfully implemented commitment and a commitment to develop, as needed.

This cycle needs to be repeated until you as a setting feel comfortable with the commitments. This can be reviewed by completing Step 1 again if you want. Ensure that all commitments are being acted upon.

Rate how well each commitment is being achieved in the setting from 1 to 5.

1	2	3	4	5
Just starting work on this commitment				Fully implementing this commitment

Card number	Title of commitment	Commitment	Question	Rating (1–5)
1.1	Child Development	Babies and young children develop in individual ways and at varying rates. Every area of development – physical, cognitive, linguistic, spiritual, social and emotional – is equally important.	Are the babies and young children allowed to develop in individual ways and at varying rates? Is every area of development – physical, cognitive, linguistic, spiritual, social and emotional – treated as equally important?	
1.2	Inclusive Practice	The diversity of individuals and communities is valued and respected. No child or family is discriminated against.	Is the diversity of individuals and communities valued and respected? Are any children or families discriminated against?	
1.3	Keeping Safe	Young children are vulnerable. They develop resilience when their physical and psychological well-being is protected by adults.	Are young children recognised as vulnerable? Is young children's physical and psychological well-being protected by adults in order that they can develop resilience?	
1.4	Health and Well-being	Children's health is an integral part of their emotional, mental, social, environmental and spiritual well-being and is supported by attention to these aspects.	Are all aspects of children's health – emotional, mental, social, environmental and spiritual recognised and supported by giving attention to these aspects?	
2.1	Respecting Each Other	Every interaction is based on caring professional relationships and respectful acknowledgement of the feelings of children and their families.	Is every interaction based on caring professional relationships and respectful acknowledgement of the feelings of children and their families?	
2.2	Parents as Partners	Parents are children's first and most enduring educators. When parents and practitioners work together in early years settings, the results have a positive impact on children's development and learning.	Are parents recognised as their child's first and most enduring educators? Do parents and practitioners work together in relation to the children's development and learning in the setting?	
2.3	Supporting Learning	Warm, trusting relationships with knowledgeable adults support children's learning more effectively than any amount of resources.	Are there warm, trusting relationships between knowledgeable adults and the children to support the children's learning?	
2.4	Key Person	A key person has special responsibilities for working with a small number of children, giving them the reassurance to feel safe and cared for and building relationships with their parents.	Is there a key person system in the setting where each key person has special responsibilities for working with a small number of children, giving them the reassurance to feel safe and cared for and building relationships with their parents?	

continued on next sheet

Rate how well each commitment is being achieved in the setting from 1 to 5.

1		2	3	4	5
Just starting work on this commitment					Fully implementing this commitment

Card number	Title of commitment	Commitment	Question	Rating (1–5)
3.1	Observation, Assessment and Planning	Babies and young children are individuals first, each with a unique profile of abilities. Schedules and routines should flow with the child's needs. All planning starts with observing children in order to understand and consider their current interests, development and learning.	Are babies and young children recognised as individuals with a unique profile of abilities? Do schedules and routines flow with the child's needs? Does the planning start with observing children and their current interests, development and learning?	
3.2	Supporting Every Child	The environment supports every child's learning through planned experiences and activities that are challenging but achievable	Does the setting's environment support every child's learning through planned experiences and activities that are challenging but achievable?	
3.3	The Learning Environment	A rich and varied environment supports children's learning and development. It gives them the confidence to explore and learn in secure and safe, yet challenging, indoor and outdoor spaces.	Has the setting got a rich and varied environment that supports children's learning and development and gives them the confidence to explore and learn in secure and safe, yet challenging, indoor and outdoor spaces?	
3.4	The Wider Context	Working in partnership with other settings, other professionals and with individuals and groups in the community supports children's development and progress towards the outcomes of *Every Child Matters*: being healthy, staying safe, enjoying and achieving, making a positive contribution and economic well-being.	Does the setting work in partnership with other settings, other professionals and with individuals and groups in the community supporting children's development and progress towards the outcomes of *Every Child Matters*: being healthy, staying safe, enjoying and achieving, making a positive contribution and economic well-being?	
4.1	Play and Exploration	Children's play reflects their wide ranging and varied interests and preoccupations. In their play children learn at their highest level. Play with peers is important for children's development.	Does children's play reflect their wide ranging and varied interests and preoccupations and allow children to learn at their highest level? Is play with peers taking place?	
4.2	Active Learning	Children learn best through physical and mental challenges. Active learning involves other people, objects, ideas and events that engage and involve children for sustained periods.	Do children have opportunities for active learning that involves other people, objects, ideas and events that engage and involve children for sustained periods?	
4.3	Creativity and Critical Thinking	When children have opportunities to play with ideas in different situations and with a variety of resources, they discover connections and come to new and better understandings and ways of doing things. Adult support in this process enhances their ability to think critically and ask questions.	Do children have opportunities to play with ideas in different situations and with a variety of resources so they discover connections and come to new and better understandings and ways of doing things? Do adults supporting this process enhance children's ability to think critically and ask questions?	

The EYFS: Am I getting it right? © Anita Soni & Sue Bristow

Your name (optional): _____   Child's name (optional): _____

Rate how well each commitment is being achieved in the setting from 1 to 5 for your child.

1	2	3	4	5
Just starting to do this				Fully doing this

Card number	Title of commitment	Question on the commitment	Rating (1–5)
1.1	Child Development	Is your child allowed to develop fully in their own way at their own rate?	
1.2	Inclusive Practice	Is your child, family and community valued and respected rather than discriminated against?	
1.3	Keeping Safe	Is your child kept safe, physically and emotionally, and protected by adults?	
1.4	Health and Well-being	Is your child's health and well-being recognised and supported by the adults in the setting?	
2.1	Respecting Each Other	Do the adults in the setting respect you, your family and your child and your feelings?	
2.2	Parents as Partners	Do the adults in the setting recognise you as your child's first and most important teacher?	
2.3	Supporting Learning	Are there warm, trusting relationships between the adults in the setting and the children? Do you think the adults are knowledgeable about your child and their job?	
2.4	Key Person	Is there someone in the setting who works to build relationships with your child and you?	
3.1	Observation, Assessment and Planning	Do the setting's ideas and activities recognise that your child is an individual with their particular interests?	
3.2	Supporting Every Child	Does the setting support your child's learning with experiences and activities that are challenging but achievable?	
3.3	The Learning Environment	Is the setting secure, safe and challenging to support your child's learning and development, both indoor and outdoor?	
3.4	The Wider Context	Does the setting work with other settings, other professionals and with individuals and groups in the community?	
4.1	Play and Exploration	Can the children play with friends and toys or objects that interest them?	
4.2	Active Learning	Does your child have opportunities to actively learn, doing things that engage and sustain him/her?	
4.3	Creativity and Critical Thinking	Do adults help your child to play with ideas and resources in different situations to discover connections and understand different ways of doing things?	

Card number	Commitment	Scores		Total
		Practitioner's	Parents'	
1.1	Child Development			
1.2	Inclusive Practice			
1.3	Keeping Safe			
1.4	Health and Well-being			
2.1	Respecting Each Other			
2.2	Parents as Partners			
2.3	Supporting Learning			
2.4	Key Person			
3.1	Observation, Assessment and Planning			
3.2	Supporting Every Child			
3.3	The Learning Environment			
3.4	The Wider Context			
4.1	Play and Exploration			
4.2	Active Learning			
4.3	Creativity and Critical Thinking			

1
Visit at home.
Detailed induction information.
Key person gets to know the family during induction.
Key person and 'Buddy' available at both ends of the day.
Key person biographies displayed.

2
Induction and moving rooms is planned at the child's pace.
Pictures of the child's family displayed in the environment.
Each child has a 'tray' for their personal things.
Minor changes are made to the room arrangement throughout the year.

3
Learning journeys are sent home every three months and parents are asked to add their observations and photographs.
Key person shares the learning journey with each key child and the child has an opportunity to add their favourite photographs and work to them.
A speech and language therapist visited a child in the room and his learning journey was shared with her.

4
Informal discussions with the staff in the room about how to support the new experience with each child.
Key person to support the new experience if possible.
Talk to child about experience beforehand and parent if necessary.

5
Jake likes to be cuddled when sad.
Shivani likes to be with best friend Anna.

6
Informal support from room leader.
Regular supervision.

7
Display on the key person role in the entrance. Key person role explained to each parent on induction and parent friendly key person policy included in induction pack.
Training for staff on the key person role.

8
Daily home and nursery communication book.
Three-monthly meetings.

9
Key person or buddy always available where possible.
Transitional objects welcomed from home as well as nursery.
See Transition form for movement between rooms.
See Room handbooks given when each child moves room.
Staff given time to move up with them and help the child make a relationship with their new key person.

A key person has special responsibilities for working with a small number of children, giving them the reassurance to feel safe and cared for and building relationships with their parents.

10
Key person training for all staff identified in key person policy.
Staff support each other as necessary.

11
Each child has a key person and a back up key person called a 'buddy'.
Rotas are planned so that where possible either staff member is available at all times.

12
See question 11.

13
Where possible the 'buddy' takes on the primary key person role and the new member of staff becomes the 'buddy'.

14
See question 11

15
Pictures of the child's family displayed in the environment.
Each child has a 'tray' for their personal things.
Cosy area is available in the room.
Resources that children recognise from home and are interested in are available in the room.

16
On the agenda for next staff meeting.

17
Home and nursery communication book.
Regular newsletters, email and texts.
Staff phone parents every three months.

18
Observe children to see how staff can plan to support 'friendships'.
Friendships are shared with parents so that parents can make links outside of nursery.
Senior management plan to spend time in rooms.
The cook visits the children every week to plan the menus.
Parents are invited in to spend time in the nursery and share their skills, such as cooking.

1	2	3	4
5	**6**	**7**	**8**
9			**10**
	Commitment		
11	**12**	**13**	**14**
15	**16**	**17**	**18**

1 Does your planning show that you start from activities relating to what children can do? Give examples.

2 How well do you know each child's characteristics and temperament? Think of each of your key children in turn. Where is this shown?

3 How do you know you allow the children to explore the resources and environment in their own way? For example, photographs of the environment.

4 How do you show you recognise how important practitioners are for the children?

5 How do you show you know the important details about each child in your key group? For example, planning; special interest sheets.

6 Do you communicate, play and spend time with all your key children every time they come to your setting? Think of each of your key children in turn.

7 Do you allow the children to communicate in many different ways by using their talk, gaze, drawing, writing, singing, dancing, music and drama? Consider evidence for verbal and non-verbal communication.

8 Do you let children do the activities and experiences rather than tell them or show them? Give an example.

9 Do you know about each of your key children's culture and background? Where does this show in the setting?

Babies and children develop in individual ways and at varying rates. Every area of development – physical, cognitive, linguistic, spiritual, social and emotional, is equally important.

10 Where do your records show that you know what each child is interested in and what makes them smile?

11 How do you let children learn and develop at their own pace and not rush them or slow them down? Give examples.

12 Do you recognise and praise children for effort as well as achievement? Give examples.

13 When do you listen and respond to verbal and non-verbal communication from the babies and children? Give examples.

14 How do you make sure that you spend time with every child 'fairly'?

15 Where in your planning and records do you show recognition of all areas of development?

16 Do you allow children to say what they want/need to say, no matter how long it takes? Give an example.

17 Where in your planning of activities and experiences are each child's interests represented?

18 How does your setting show it has a key person system for each child and his/her parents?

1 Do you smile, welcome and listen to all the families? Think of each of your families in your key group in turn.	**2** Where do you show that you include children from socially excluded families such as the homeless, or those who live with a parent who is disabled or has a mental illness? For example, a display.	**3** Where do you show that you include children from traveller communities, refugees, asylum seekers and those from diverse linguistic backgrounds? For example, a policy.	**4** Where do you show that you include children who are disabled and those who have special educational needs? For example, play resources.
5 How do you keep your knowledge about religions and different cultural groups up to date?	**6** How do you allow children to develop as individuals with their own cultural and spiritual beliefs?	**7** When do you reflect on your attitudes to people who are different to you?	**8** When do you ask parents whether any specialist services or equipment are needed for children who need additional support?
9 Do you treat all children fairly regardless of their race, religion, abilities, what they think or do, the languages they speak, what their parents do and whether they have a disability or their social background? Where is this recorded?	**The diversity of individuals and communities is valued and respected. No child or family is discriminated against.**		**10** How do you take part in sensitive two-way exchange of information with all families?
11 How do you listen to all children and show that you value what they have to say?	**12** How do you ensure you identify children who need additional support as early as possible so that they can get the help they need?	**13** Do you have records that are suitable for sharing with other agencies, for example, health visitors, speech and language therapists?	**14** Do you have displays, objects and photographs that relate to the families who use the setting?
15 Do you plan jointly with everyone who is in contact with children who have severe and complex support needs, for example, families and other professionals? Where is this recorded?	**16** Do you know when and how to call in specialist support for children and families? How would you find out?	**17** How do you encourage children to recognise their own unique qualities and the characteristics they share with other children? For example, displays.	**18** Where do your displays and photographs show the names of the staff and welcome children from a variety of cultures and languages?

1 Where are the clear limits on what children may and may not do recorded, for example, signs, policy? Are they reinforced consistently by all practitioners?	**2** Do you explain the rules, boundaries and limits to the children in a way that they can understand? Give an example.	**3** How do you encourage children to contribute to deciding what are the limits, rules and boundaries so they understand them?	**4** How do you work with parents to have consistent boundaries for behaviour at home and in the setting?
5 How do you keep an open and flexible dialogue with parents and professionals whose views about child-rearing or behaviour are different to yours?	**6** What stories do you read about everyday events so children know who to trust and how to keep safe? When do you talk about this?	**7** How do you help children to assertively say no when needed?	**8** Do you listen to what children tell you and act on non-verbal signals especially from children who are anxious? Give examples.
9 Do you let children choose not to join in even if they are the only one to do so? Give an example.	Young children are vulnerable. They develop resilience when their physical and psychological well-being is protected by adults.		**10** Do you explain to the children why they are allowed to choose and times when they are not allowed? Give examples of how you give children choices so they learn to choose and help themselves?
11 How do you encourage children to make choices over what they wear or do, to give them some sense of control?	**12** When do you let children do things for themselves and still give an appropriate level of support where needed?	**13** Do you encourage, listen and respond to verbal and non-verbal communication from babies and children? Give examples.	**14** What activities and experiences do you give that help children know how to recognise and avoid possible danger and think about ways to keep safe?
15 What activities and experiences do you provide that help children feel good about themselves?	**16** What activities and experiences for the children are about people who help them?	**17** When do you let children have time to think about what they want and express that rather than making decisions for them?	**18** When do you help and show children how you assess the risks in the setting?

1 How do you ensure the children are safe without stopping reasonable risk taking?

2 How do you encourage the children to move around the room to different activities and resources as they play?

3 How do you help children to understand why some choices in food and drink are healthier than others?

4 Do you know how to recognise child abuse and neglect? Who do you consult if there is a cause for concern? How do you record this?

5 Do you plan that babies and children with special needs access similar opportunities to their peers? Give an example.

6 Do all the children have a close relationship with their key person? How do you do this? Is this reviewed regularly?

7 Are the children encouraged to join in and help with manageable tasks around the setting? Give an example.

8 How do you encourage parents and grandparents to share their knowledge of their child with you?

9 How do you create relationships with the children that are close, warm and supportive?

Children's health is an integral part of their emotional, mental, social, environmental and spiritual well-being and is supported by attention to these aspects.

10 When do the children have access to the outdoors?

11 What is in place to ensure the environment is clean and safe?

12 How well do you know the care routines for feeding, toileting and sleeping for each individual child? Think of each of your key children in turn.

13 Do you present food and items from other cultures as an every day experience within the setting not as a novelty? Give an example.

14 How do you encourage the children to make friends and play with each other?

15 Is there a balance of activities so children can be involved, and rest and relax at different times? Where are the places for children to sleep, rest or relax?

16 How are the parents involved in promoting their child's health and well-being in the setting? Are their photographs displayed or are they asked to bring in resources?

17 How do you help children know about the food chain? Do you plant, grow and use the foods grown with the children?

18 Where are the large, interesting spaces for energetic movement indoors and outdoors?

1 How do you show that you recognise the feelings of the adults and children in the setting?	**2** How do you show that you respect and value the strengths, skills and knowledge of the people that you work with?	**3** How is each child, parent and practitioner valued for who they are and their differences appreciated?	**4** How do you support the children in making friends with each other?
5 How do you support the children who are shy or find it difficult to interact or to make friends?	**6** How do you help children who find it difficult to get on and play with others and be friendly?	**7** How do you ensure you work in partnership with parents and are friendly but maintain a professional distance?	**8** When do you recognise and label the feelings expressed by the children, including those that can be more challenging like anger?
9 When do you allow the children to practically help and emotionally support each other?	**Every interaction is based on caring professional relationships and respectful acknowledgement of the feelings of children and their families.**		**10** How are the contributions of each person recognised in your setting?
11 In your setting, how do you show you make best use of the people available to best meet the needs of the children?	**12** How do you deal with strong feelings or personal prejudices about an issue that may be a barrier to supporting a child and their family?	**13** How does communication at the setting include everyone's views while keeping the needs of the children firmly in mind?	**14** When do you listen to parents' feelings, concerns and views?
15 Are you aware that different factors will affect children's and families' ability to be friendly?	**16** How does the setting support mutual respect between staff members themselves?	**17** How does the setting support mutual respect between parents and children?	**18** How does the setting support mutual respect between staff and children?

1 How do you ensure all families are welcomed and valued in your setting?

2 How do you greet children and parents in the setting? Are these greetings used at home by families in your setting?

3 Do you show recognition of the different types of families in your displays, books, photographs, posters? Give examples.

4 How do you create an atmosphere at the setting that allows communication between parents and the setting?

5 Give examples of the two-way flow of information, knowledge and expertise between parents and practitioners?

6 How do you support parents in understanding more about learning and teaching on areas such as play, outdoor learning, early reading and so on?

7 How do you give opportunities for parents to review their child's progress regularly and contribute to their child's learning and development record?

8 How do you show you value the different home languages used by children in the setting?

9 When and how do you create opportunities for informal talk with parents?

Parents are children's first and most enduring educators. When parents and practitioners work together in early years settings, the results have a positive impact on children's development and learning.

10 When do you involve parents in writing words from their home language, for example, to use in displays, books and so on?

11 As a staff member, when do you talk about diversity, equality and anti-oppressive practice?

12 How do you seek the views of parents on the care and education provided in the setting?

13 How can the parents of the children communicate with the setting, for example, daily books?

14 Give examples of the way your setting 'communicates' with parents who are busy or working.

15 How does the setting recognise and value the role played by parents in developing their child's learning and development?

16 How do you ensure the parents understand and contribute to the setting's policies in key areas such as learning and teaching, inclusion and behaviour?

17 Do you run/signpost family learning courses and other opportunities for parents to access learning?

18 How do you get fathers and male family members involved in the setting?

1

What does each child like to do?
When is each child confident, scared or frustrated?
Think of each key child in turn.

2

How do you use your observations to encourage and extend the children's learning?

3

How do you motivate and encourage children to persist and try several ways to make things work rather than giving up at the first attempt?

4

What do you do to ensure that children are given time and space to respond?

5

How do you build respectful, caring relationships with all the children and families while focusing on learning and achievement?

6

How do you ensure you listen to babies and younger children who have a delay in their speech or who speak English as an additional language?

7

Give examples of different ways you help the children make connections in their learning.

8

When do you model being a learner with the children, for example, by talking about the problem and asking the children to help solve it?

9

How do you encourage children to reflect on their learning?

Warm, trusting relationships with knowledgeable adults support children's learning more effectively than any amount of resources.

10

What examples can you give of following the children's lead in play?

11

How do you help each child to know you are genuinely pleased to see them each day?

12

How do you make sure activities, stories and play experiences are pitched at the right level for each child?

13

When have you listened to and acted on children's views that don't match your own? Give examples.

14

Who are the children you find more difficult to build positive relationships with and how could you get to know them better?

15

How do you help the children feel confident to try new things and take on challenges?

16

How do you ensure that you intervene in children's learning at the right time rather than dominate it?

17

How often do you record yourself in a group activity, and then reflect on who talks the most and what sort of talk it is?

18

Give examples of when you actively listen and respond to children.

1 In what ways do you build a genuine bond with each child and their family?

2 How do you help your key children become familiar with the environment and feel safe in it?

3 How do you ensure that each key child's records of progress and development are created and shared by parents, the child, the key person and other professionals?

4 How do you support the children in exploring new experiences and activities?

5 How do you ensure you respond sensitively to each of your key children's feelings, ideas and behaviour?
Consider each of your key children in turn.

6 What support is available for practitioners who start to feel too attached to a key child?

7 How do you reassure staff and parents that children will not become too dependent on their key person?

8 Do you talk to parents of your key children regularly so you know how to care for them? How often does this happen?

9 How do you support children and parents in transitions? Are they given time with and information about their new key person when they move rooms or settings?

A key person has special responsibilities for working with a small number of children, giving them the reassurance to feel safe and cared for and building relationships with their parents.

10 Do you recognise that children and babies are likely to be less independent when in new situations or when unwell or anxious? How do you support this?

11 How do you ensure that each child can be reassured and comforted by key adults at times they may need it?

12 Who is the key person for each child? When does the key person 'spend' time with each key child?

13 How do you support children's transitions between key person relationships in the setting when there are staff changes?

14 Who is the back-up key person for each child for when the key person is away for breaks, courses, holiday and so on?

15 How do you help the setting feel familiar and comfortable for each child especially any new ones?

16 Do you reflect on how your setting might feel to different parents and children?
How is this achieved?

17 How do you communicate with parents of your key children who are very busy and don't have time to talk?

18 How do you support children to make relationships with other children and other adults?

1
Do you know what each child needs, is interested in and can do?
Think of each of your key children in turn.

2
How does your planning show how you support each child's learning and development?

3
What do you know about the Common Assessment Framework (CAF) for children with additional needs so you can be involved as needed?
Are there any areas you would like further explanation of?

4
When do you analyse your observations to consider who needs more support and who has achieved something new?
Do you do this alone or in conjunction with others?

5
Where are the assessments of children's learning and development and can the children and parents access them?

6
Are your records clear and accessible for everybody to understand including the child and parents?

7
How do you ensure that parents have regular opportunities to add to their child's learning and development record?

8
How do you involve parents in the ongoing observation and assessment process?

9
Where are the views of the parents shown in the children's records?

Babies and young children are individuals first, each with a unique profile of abilities. Schedules and routines should flow with the child's needs. All planning starts with observing children in order to understand and consider their current interests, development and learning.

10
How do you involve busy or working parents in observing and planning for their children?

11
Do you observe children in different situations and at different times of their day?

12
How do you ensure you observe children who attend the setting on an irregular basis?

13
Is your planning flexible so the children can learn from spontaneous events such as a fall of snow?

14
How does your planning reflect each of your child's interests?
Think of each of your key children in turn.

15
How do you ensure you observe as a part of the daily routine?

16
How do you show the ideas on your planning come from observing the children and analysing these observations?

17
How and when do you review a child's level of involvement in different activities to help you plan?

18
Do you review your environment and resources during or after each session as part of your planning?

1 How do you know when to support children and when to step back?

2 How do you make sure you follow every child's individual interests and needs in their learning?

3 How do you ensure you give some new and interesting challenges?

4 How do you ensure that you offer a range of experiences to the children, including some that are comforting, familiar and predictable?

5 How do you ensure that the children are always able to have their physical needs met? Consider their needs for food, water, sleep and rest?

6 How do you work with the child's parents to achieve the best for each child?

7 How do you ensure you listen to children's needs in the learning process?

8 How do you involve people from the wider community in children's learning?

9 How do you communicate with other settings a child may go to at the same time, or have been to or will go to?

The environment supports every child's learning through planned experiences and activities that are challenging but achievable.

10 How can you make the most ordinary events such as going to the toilet, setting the table and getting ready to go home, more exciting and interesting for the children?

11 Can you give examples of how you provide appropriate, realistic experiences that build on children's interests?

12 Can you give examples of how you bring children's experiences of home into the learning?

13 How do you keep your planning for individual children realistic while keeping a focus on broader learning outcomes in *Development matters in the EYFS*?

14 Give examples of how you have extended a child's special talents and things they are good at.

15 How do you ensure that the children are always able to have their emotional needs met? Consider the need for a hug, encouragement or reassurance.

16 How does the setting make sure that what is written in a policy happens in reality day-to-day?

17 How do you work with other professionals who may be involved with one of your key children to achieve the best for this child?

18 How do you involve the children in making choices about planned experiences and activities?

1 How do you create a warm and accepting emotional environment at the setting?	**2** How do you show you empathise with the children and encourage them all to express their emotions?	**3** How do you create an indoor environment that is reassuring and comforting for the children but still provide interest and novelty?	**4** How do you show the children that you accept all their emotions not just happiness and joy?
5 What support is there for practitioners who may feel drained when a child requires high levels of support for their strong feelings of sadness, anger or frustration?	**6** How do you ensure that you allow children to have first-hand contact with different weathers and seasons and aspects of the natural world?	**7** How do you involve children in planning the layout of the room so they are more likely to respect it and keep it tidy?	**8** How do you give children the best opportunity to learn outdoors on a daily basis as well as indoors?
9 How do you promote the importance and value of outdoor play to all those involved in the setting including parents and staff?	A rich and varied environment supports children's learning and development. It gives them confidence to explore and learn in secure and safe, yet challenging, indoor and outdoor spaces.		**10** How do you help children to understand how to behave outdoors and inside?
11 How do you encourage the children to experience learning both inside and outside?	**12** How well do you reflect examples of outdoor learning as well as indoor learning in your observations and assessments?	**13** How do you ensure deployment of staff is flexible enough to respond to the flow and movement of children between indoors and outdoors?	**14** How do you encourage the children to link indoor and outdoor environments?
15 How do you show you value children's efforts rather than just their achievements and products?	**16** How do you adapt and plan your indoor environment and spaces to make best use of them and provide a range of activities?	**17** How do you develop the indoor environment to be 'homely' for the children but still promote learning?	**18** How do you ensure your resources are appropriate, well maintained and accessible for the children?

1 How do you effectively communicate with any other settings each child attends?

2 How do you effectively communicate with previous settings the child has attended or a future setting?

3 How do you share the children's records of development and learning with other settings the child may attend?

4 How do you support children and parents with transition times, for example, start/end of day and changes of rooms, especially those who find it stressful?

5 How do you show you value what parents tell you about their child on induction?

6 How do you involve parents in transition times such as induction and settling in times and in other decisions about their child?

7 How do you keep parents informed in advance of what will happen at transition times such as when children join the setting?

8 Do you have a policy for transition shared with everyone involved in and beyond the setting?

9 How do you help children and families who are new to the area or your setting to settle in and get to know people?

Working in partnership with other settings, other professionals and with individuals and groups in the community supports children's development and progress towards the outcomes of *Every Child Matters*: being healthy, staying safe, enjoying and achieving, making a positive contribution and economic well-being.

10 How do you ensure you put the child's needs first when you work with other agencies, for example, health visitors, speech therapists?

11 What other agencies do you work with to help children achieve the *Every Child Matters* outcomes: being healthy; staying safe; enjoying and achieving; making a positive contribution and achieving economic well-being?

12 How do ensure you value and respect colleagues from other professional backgrounds?

13 How do you make your records of children's learning and development accessible and easy to share with other agencies?

14 How do you use the local community to support the children's learning?

15 How do you and the setting work to make links with other early years provision in the local community?

16 How do you get members of the local community to share their expertise (for example, gardening, storytelling) and get involved in the setting?

17 How do you and the setting show you value the local community?

18 How well do you and other staff know the local area and how much do you use this knowledge in planning for children's learning?

The EYFS: Am I getting it right? © Anita Soni & Sue Bristow

1 Where can children choose to play alone in the setting?

2 Where can children play with other children? How do you encourage children to play either in parallel or together?

3 Where can children role play and act out things they may be worried about like monsters, new babies, the doctors?

4 Do children get the chance to play indoors and outdoors every day? How often?

5 Do you let children play where they can solve problems, take risks and find things out themselves? Give an example.

6 Can the children play with resources and equipment before trying to solve a problem with them? Give an example.

7 How do you develop children's language and communication when playing with them?

8 When do you plan activities for children to play with in their own way, where the end result may be different for every child? Give an example from your planning.

9 Can the children make dens and play dressing-up?

Children's play reflects their wide ranging and varied interests and preoccupations. In their play children learn at their highest level. Play with peers is important for children's development.

10 When have you told or read stories for children to act out themselves?

11 Where can the children access role-play resources of their choice?

12 Do you challenge any play that is racist, sexist, offensive, unsafe or violent? Give an example.

13 When have you allowed play based on superheroes and other ideas that mean a lot to children even if they don't mean much to you?

14 Do you observe and watch before deciding to join in with children's play? Give an example.

15 What flexible resources do you have that can be used in many different ways? For example, fabric and pegs, boxes, clothes horses, blankets and tablecloths?

16 How are the parents involved in the setting and the children's play? Do you have parents' photographs up? Or do you ask them to bring in resources?

17 Do you base play on themes that the children may like even if you don't? Give an example.

18 How do you know how children like to play at home?

1 Are all the children at ease, secure and confident? How do you know?

2 When do you challenge and extend the children's thinking? Give an example.

3 Do you know the activities each child gets mostly involved in? Think of each key child in turn.

4 When do you find out from parents what activities and play their child gets most involved with at home?

5 How do you let children control and make decisions about their play and learning? When do children make choices about what they use, and how it looks at the end?

6 How are the children's learning journeys shared with the child, their parents and peers? For example, through displays, records, and photographs?

7 How and when do you review your environment to ensure it is interesting, accessible and attractive to every child within it?

8 How do you promote children investigating and exploring new ideas for themselves?

9 How do you ensure every child's learning journey is unique from other children's?

Children learn best through physical and mental challenges. Active learning involves other people, objects, ideas and events that engage and involve children for sustained periods.

10 When do you encourage the children to ask questions?

11 How do you make sure that your expectations are realistic for each child?

12 Where does your planning reflect the interests and learning of each child?

13 When do you analyse and reflect on what has been observed to show what children have learned?

14 Do the children have time, space and independence in their own learning to follow their own ideas and what they are interested in? Where and when?

15 How do you consider how long children are involved in their learning and use this information in planning? Give an example from planning.

16 How do you keep the learning active for each child?

17 When do you look at the nature and quality of adult interactions in children's learning? For example, evaluations?

18 How do you show that your planning comes from your observations and information from talking to the child and from their parents?

1 How do you show that you value children's home lives/culture? Do you let them share items from home?

2 How do you develop individual creativity in children? Give an example of an open-ended activity.

3 How do you help children make connections between experiences? When do they have opportunities to repeat experiences in different ways?

4 How do you recognise the process of being creative? For example, through recording observations or by taking photographs of the process?

5 When do you let children play with the process, for example, glue and paper, before expecting them to make products like cards?

6 When and how do you show genuine interest in, encourage and clarify children's ideas to support their thinking?

7 Do you model being creative in your thinking of ideas and making creative items? Give an example.

8 How do you share the observations and photographs with the children? When do you re-visit learning and reflect on the child's thinking?

9 How do you know what each child is interested in and understands? How do you work with this information to develop them further?

When children have opportunities to play with ideas in different situations and with a variety of resources, they discover connections and come to new and better understandings and ways of doing things. Adult support in this process enhances their ability to think critically and ask questions.

10 How do you support and challenge children's thinking and ideas? Have you ever taped your interactions with children to see how you support their development of creativity and critical thinking?

11 Where do you record how children's thinking develops? When do you share the photographs and observations with parents?

12 How do you find out about and value children's learning and behaviour from their parents? How do you find out how they behave at home and support this?

13 How do you ensure that you have a balance of adult-led and child-initiated activities?

14 Do you allow the children to take things from one area to another, indoor and outdoor, so they can make connections? Give an example. At the same time how do you ensure they understand the importance of looking after their things and tidying up?

15 What kind of open questions do you ask? Give an example.

16 When do you let children express their ideas in different ways: movement, dance, drawing and writing. How do you show that you value each one equally?

17 When can children choose to repeat activities and experiences as many times as they want? Give an example.

18 When can children produce their own creation rather than everyone's being the same?

EYFS focus

e.g. Area of Learning and Development or Commitment

What are you going to do?	How are you going to do it?	Who?	When?	Resources?	How will you know when this action has been achieved?

The Characteristics of Effective Learning

The *Development Matters in the EYFS* (Dfe, 2012) has emphasised the three Characteristics of Effective Learning as:

- Playing and exploring
- Active learning
- Creating and critical thinking

These three Characteristics of Effective Learning are viewed as interconnected with the seven areas of Learning and Development.

The three Prime areas of:

- Personal, social and emotional development
- Communication and Language
- Physical Development

The four Specific areas of:

- Literacy
- Mathematics
- Understanding of the world
- Expressive arts and design

These characteristics build further on the three Principles into Practice Commitment cards

- 4.1 Play and Exploration
- 4.2 Active Learning
- 4.3 Creativity and Critical Thinking

Therefore these have been developed into practitioner questionnaires with a similar pattern to those for the areas of Learning and Development on pages 53–104. The practitioner questionnaires ask practitioners to evaluate:

- Their knowledge of their key children (Unique Child principle)
- Their practice with the children (Positive Relationships principle)
- Their environment (Enabling Environments principle)

The practitioner questionnaires that follow are:

- Effective learning – Playing and Exploring questionnaire
- Effective learning – Active Learning questionnaire
- Effective learning – Creating and Thinking Critically questionnaire

THE UNIQUENESS OF YOUR CHILDREN – How much do you know about the children in your key group?

Do you know....	Yes	Where is the evidence?	No
The activities and experiences that each child likes to find out about and explore?			
What play does each child enjoy and return to?			
Where in the environment or in which experiences does each child show a willingness to have a go?			
Who can select appropriate resources and adapts work where necessary?			

POSITIVE RELATIONSHIPS – What do you do?

Do you....	Yes	When or where?	No
Play with the children, encourage them to explore?			
Support the children without taking over or directing?			
Follow the child's lead in how they want to play?			
Help develop roles and stories with the children?			
Encourage children to try new activities?			
Observe how children engage in activities their thought, learning, effort and enjoyment?			
Talk about how adults and children get better at things through effort and practice?			

ENABLING ENVIRONMENTS – Do you have?

Do you have.....	Yes	Where?	No
Stimulating resources which are accessible and open-ended so they can be used in different ways?			
Resources that support children's interests?			
Flexible indoor and outdoor space and resources to enable exploration, building and role play?			
Reduced background noise so children can concentrate?			
An orderly and calm environment?			
First hand experiences at the appropriate level for the children?			
Uninterrupted time for the children to play and explore?			

If you have ticked no to any question, use this as a basis to complete an action plan as on page 40 to identify what you need to find out more about and how to develop your practice or environment.

THE UNIQUENESS OF YOUR CHILDREN – How much do you know about the children in your key group?

Do you know....	Yes	Where is the evidence?	No
The activities and experiences that involve each child and they maintain focus on for a period of time?			
When is each child most likely to persist or keep trying?			
When does each child show enjoyment in achieving what they have set out to do?			

POSITIVE RELATIONSHIPS – What do you do?

Do you....	Yes	When or where?	No
Support children to make choices in the activities they want to do and how to do it?			
Respond to children's engagement levels by calming over stimulated children and seeking to stimulate less engaged children?			
Encourage children to know how well they are progressing?			
Give specific praise based on children's efforts during the process rather than the product?			
Encourage to children to help each other and learn together?			
Encourage children by explaining why you are offering an experience and the learning?			
Help children recognise their own successes?			

ENABLING ENVIRONMENTS – Do you have?

Do you have.....	Yes	Where?	No
New and unusual resources that are linked to children's interests?			
Experiences and activities based on what you have observed children being deeply involved in?			
Time and freedom for children to become deeply involved in activities?			
Photographs of previous activities to help children make links between previous experiences?			
Continuation of significant activities over time rather than tidying away too quickly?			
Space and time for all children to contribute in their own way?			

If you have ticked no to any question, use this as a basis to complete an action plan as on page 40 to identify what you need to find out more about and how to develop your practice or environment.

THE UNIQUENESS OF YOUR CHILDREN – How much do you know about the children in your key group?

Do you know....	Yes	Where is the evidence?	No
When each child is confident of their own ideas?			
When does each child make links between different things they experience at home and at the setting?			
When is each child most able to choose their own way of doing things?			

POSITIVE RELATIONSHIPS – What do you do?

Do you....	Yes	When or where?	No
Use the language of thinking and learning e.g. working out, trying out ideas?			
Role model thinking and trying out different ways of doing things?			
Encourage children to give their ideas and thoughts?			
Encourage children to have a go by valuing their effort?			
Model self-talk, describing what you are doing as you do it to show your thinking?			
Give time for children to think and talk things over?			
Gradually move towards answers, rather than rushing through ideas?			
Encourage children's interests to develop by reminding them of previous similar experiences?			
Follow children's lead in their conversation and ideas?			
Encourage children to think of their own solutions?			
Give feedback on how each child is progressing and learning?			

ENABLING ENVIRONMENTS – Do you have?

Do you have.....	Yes	Where?	No
Planned activities and experiences where children can find their own ways to represent their ideas?			
Opportunities for children to play with resources and materials before using them in planned activities?			
Time, space, flexible resources, choice and control within warm key person relationships to allow children to develop rich play?			
Predictable routines that help children make links between their experiences?			
Planned experiences that follow the children's ideas?			
Mind-maps to show the joint planning and thinking with children?			
A learning community where everyone at the setting is reflecting on how learning happens, rather than what is learned?			

If you have ticked no to any question, use this as a basis to complete an action plan as on page 40 to identify what you need to find out more about and how to develop your practice or environment.

STAGE 4

The seven areas of Learning and Development

Once your setting has reflected upon the Principles into Practice card, the commitments within it, and the Characteristics of Effective Learning, the next stage is to consider the areas of Learning and Development. This is within the last section of the Principles into Practice Commitment card and needs reflecting upon in the same way as the other commitments.

However there is much more to consider as there are links to the seven areas of Learning and Development and the *Development Matters in the EYFS*. To begin to evaluate your practice within the Areas of Learning and Development follow the step-by-step approach below.

STEP 1   All staff (and possibly parents) to complete the Areas of Learning and Development questionnaire.

The questionnaire is presented using the educational programmes described in the *Statutory Framework for the EYFS*. There are two versions, one for practitioners and one for parents:

● The questionnaire for practitioners provides a statement about each area of Learning and Development and a question for practitioners to consider (see page 48). They should rank how well they feel the setting is doing on each area of Learning and Development by using the simple scale below:

1	2	3	4	5

Just starting work on this area   Fully implementing this area
of Learning and Development   of Learning and Development

Ask staff to consider this in relation to which of the following three broad age bands they are working with: 0–20 months; 16–36 months; 30–60+ months.

● The questionnaire for parents provides simple questions about the educational programme for each Area of Learning and Development (see pages 49–50). They can rate how well they think the setting is doing by ticking various aspects of the curriculum.

When self-evaluating it will be important to emphasise that high marks are not the order of the day but that it is important that everyone is honest about the practice in the setting and is willing and open to reflect on change. It is easier to complete this quickly and not spend too long on considering each section in great depth as this is meant as a quick overview, and there is opportunity for detailed discussion later.

Photocopy one questionnaire per staff member/parent. Ask each person to fill in a questionnaire and then compile the results in the table (see below and page 51). Write the scores (1, 2, 3, 4, 5) in the third column for each person who has completed the questionnaire and then total them in the final column of the table.

Area of Learning and Development	Scores			Total
	0–20 months	16–36 months	30–60+ months	
Communication and Language				
Physical Development				
Personal, Social and Emotional Development				
Literacy				
Mathematics				
Understanding the World				
Expressive Arts and Design				

STEP 2 Analyse the completed questionnaires and identify an area of Learning and Development to celebrate and one to work on.

We suggest, initially, identifying two out of the seven areas of Learning and Development:

● One that is a strength for the setting and should be celebrated;
● One that requires some work.

This is done by totalling the scores each area of Learning and Development has been given by each person and then seeing which area has come top with the highest score, and which has come at the bottom with the lowest score.

The area of Learning and Development with the highest score is the one everyone feels is being implemented most confidently; the one with the lowest score is the one that people understand the least or feel least confident with.

This may vary from age band to age band. It may be that in your setting the staff in the baby room (working with children aged 0–20 months) are unsure of Mathematics but for pre-school (30–60+ months) Personal, Social and Emotional Development is an area to consider. Therefore the area of Learning and Development that you choose to focus on needs to come from your analysis. Alternatively if your setting only covers one age band (30–60+ months) you need only focus on this.

STEP 3 Celebrate success in an area of Learning and Development.

Choose the highest scoring area of Learning and Development. This is one that the setting is doing well so celebrate! Make a display or book to demonstrate to yourself, children, parents and Ofsted that you are already doing this part of the EYFS well. This is important! It might be tempting to overlook those areas of Learning and Development that the setting is implementing successfully, but celebrating good practice is vital for the morale and confidence of staff, parents and children.

STEP 4 Reflect on a second area of Learning and Development to improve further by evaluating the appropriate area of Learning and Development questionnaires from Step 1. Complete Key Questions questionnaires.

Choose the area of Learning and Development that scores the lowest; this is the one that requires some attention. Reflect on this area of Learning and Development by asking everyone to now complete the more detailed Key Questions questionnaires (see pages 53–104) which focus on specific aspects of the areas of Learning and Development. There are three sheets for each area of Learning and Development, covering the three age bands:

● 0–20 months
● 16–36 months
● 30–60+ months

The questionnaires ask practitioners to evaluate:

● Their knowledge of their key children (Unique Child principle)
● Their practice with the children (Positive relationships principle)
● Their environment (Enabling Environments principle)

The questionnaires for each area of Learning and Development follow the same format. See the sample completed Key questions questionnaire on page 52. This Key questions questionnaire helps you to check that you know all about the Personal, Social and Emotional Development of each of your key children.

The questionnaire should be photocopied by each practitioner to review their group of key children, their practice with them and the environment they provide for them. Observations of your key child, talking to other staff and talking to your key child's parents/carers may be a helpful way of finding out any missing information.

STEP 5   Begin to act upon the practitioner questionnaire results, develop practice further, collect evidence to show how this is being implemented.

Analyse the responses in the practitioner questionnaires, develop practice further by looking at the gaps identified by staff and decide on actions to fill the gaps identified. A photocopiable Action plan can be found on page 40. As actions are completed collect the evidence to show that the actions taken have been successful so that a display or book can be developed to celebrate the improvements made. This can be shared with staff, children, parents and Ofsted.

STEP 6   Repeat the relevant steps with a different successfully implemented area of Learning and Development and one to develop as needed. Ensure all areas of Learning and Development are being acted upon.

Ideas for development of practice can come from a number of sources including discussion with other practitioners and reflection; the relevant area of Learning and Development in the *Development Matters in the EYFS* and other information from the Foundation Years website and beyond.

Circle age group working with: 0–20 months   16–36 months   30–60 +months

Rate the setting on how far you have got with each area of Learning and Development:

1	2	3	4	5

Just starting work on this area
of Learning and Development

Fully implementing this area
of Learning and Development

Area of Learning and Development	Rating (1–5)
COMMUNICATION AND LANGUAGE **Communication and language** development involves giving children opportunities to experience a rich language environment; to develop their confidence and skills in expressing themselves; and to speak and listen in a range of situations. How well are children encouraged to develop their confidence and skills to communicate in different situations? How rich in language is the environment?	
PHYSICAL DEVELOPMENT **Physical development** involves providing opportunities for young children to be active and interactive; and to develop their co-ordination, control, and movement. Children must also be helped to understand the importance of physical activity, and to make healthy choices in relation to food. How well do the active and interactive experiences help the children develop skills of coordination, control and movement? How much are the children helped to understand the importance of physical activity and healthy food?	
PERSONAL SOCIAL AND EMOTIONAL DEVELOPMENT **Personal, social and emotional development** involves helping children to develop a positive sense of themselves, and others; to form positive relationships and develop respect for others; to develop social skills and learn how to manage their feelings; to understand appropriate behaviour in groups; and to have confidence in their own abilities How well do the experiences and support given to the children help them feel confident, good about themselves and others, form positive relationships, respect others, develop social skills and learn how to manage their feelings and behaviour?	
LITERACY **Literacy** development involves encouraging children to link sounds and letters and to begin to read and write. Children must be given access to a wide range of reading materials (books, poems, and other written materials) to ignite their interest. How well do the experiences offered to the children help them understand sounds, letters and begin to learn to read and write? How much exciting reading material is available to interest them? How well do the experiences offered to the children help them understand sounds, letters and begin to learn to read and write? How much exciting reading material is available to interest them?	
MATHEMATICS **Mathematics** involves providing children with opportunities to develop and improve their skills in counting, understanding and using numbers, calculating simple addition and subtraction problems; and to describe shapes, spaces, and measures. How much do the opportunities allow children to develop and improve their skills in counting, understanding and using numbers, calculating and to describing shape, space and measures?	
UNDERSTANDING THE WORLD **Understanding the world** involves guiding children to make sense of their physical world and their community through opportunities to explore, observe and find out about people, places, technology and the environment. How much do the opportunities given to children allow them to explore and observe different people, places, technology and the environment? How much do children get to explore and observe their physical world and community?	
EXPRESSIVE ARTS AND DESIGN **Expressive arts and design** involves enabling children to explore and play with a wide range of media and materials, as well as providing opportunities and encouragement for sharing their thoughts, ideas and feelings through a variety of activities in art, music, movement, dance, role-play, and design and technology. How much are children encouraged to explore and play with a range of media and materials? How well are they encouraged to share their ideas and feelings in a variety of art, music, movement, dance, role-play activities, design and technology?	

Please rate how well the setting is doing on each area of Learning and Development by ticking whether you feel each section is being covered:

Area of Learning and Development	Total out of 5

COMMUNICATION AND LANGUAGE

How varied and positive are the experiences and opportunities given to your child to develop skills in:

1. Communicating
2. Speaking and listening

How much is your child spoken and listened to?

Any comments on your child's development of Communication and language?

PHYSICAL DEVELOPMENT

How much do the experiences offered help your child to develop:

1. Co-ordination and control skills
2. Movement skills
3. An understanding of the importance of physical activity and healthy food?

How often does your child get the opportunity to be active?

Any comments on your child's development of physical skills?

PERSONAL SOCIAL AND EMOTIONAL DEVELOPMENT

How varied and positive are the experiences and activities given to your child to develop in:

1. Feeling good and confident about himself or herself
2. Respect for others
3. Relationships with others
4. Social skills
5. Understanding feelings
6. Manage their behaviour

Any comment on your child's development personally, socially and emotionally?

LITERACY

How varied are the opportunities for your child to learn about:

1. Sounds and letters
2. Beginning to read and write

How much exciting reading material is there for your child?

Any comment on your child's development in Literacy?

Please rate how well the setting is doing on each area of Learning and Development by ticking whether you feel each section is being covered:

Area of Learning and Development	Total out of 5

MATHEMATICS

How much do the opportunities given to your child encourage them to:

1. Count, use and understand numbers
2. Calculate simple problems
3. Describe shapes, space and measures?

Any comments on your child's development of Mathematics?

UNDERSTANDING THE WORLD

How much do the opportunities given to your child allow them to:

1. Explore their physical world and community
2. Explore a range of technology and the environment
3. Explore a range of people and places

Any comments on your child's Understanding of the World?

EXPRESSIVE ARTS AND DESIGN

How much is your child encouraged to:

1. Explore and play with a wide range of media and materials
2. Share their ideas and feelings in a variety of art, music, movement, dance and role play activities
3. Explore design and technology?

Any comment on your child's Creative Development?

Area of Learning and Development	Scores			Total
	0–20 months	16–36 months	30–60+ months	
Communication and Language				
Physical Development				
Personal, Social and Emotional Development				
Literacy				
Mathematics				
Understanding the World				
Expressive Arts and Design				

THE UNIQUENESS OF YOUR CHILDREN – How much do you know about the children in your key group?

Do you know....	Yes	Where is the evidence?	No
When each child is likely to need to check in for security?	✓	Practitioner observation	
What type of pretend play each child enjoys?	✓	Photograph	
The things each child likes to do independently?	✓	Observation	
Each child's preferences and interests?	✓	Practitioner knowledge	

POSITIVE RELATIONSHIPS – What do you do?

Do you....	Yes	When or where?	No
Model and join in pretend play?	✓	Photograph	
Have secure key person relationships with your key children?	✓	Supervision notes Parent feedback	
Encourage and support the children to try to do things independently?	✓	Self serve tea	
Respond to children's changing interests and preferences?	✓	Evaluation of planning	
Talk to children about choices they make?	✓	Accessible toys	
Know when each child may need more support?	✓	Transition paperwork	
Recognise each child's efforts by high fives or praise etc?	✓	Child's comment	

ENABLING ENVIRONMENTS – Do you have?

Do you have.....	Yes	Where?	No
Ways children can express their choices e.g. for toys, activities, snacks?	✓	Choice photograph system	
Photographs of the key people (staff) accessible to the children and parents?	✓	Display board	
Photographs of children playing to support talk about activities?	✓	Photograph books in book corner	
Time to talk with parents and each other about how each child responds to activities, adults and other children?	✓	Room meeting notes Parent partnership policy	
Records of each child's achievements and progress at the setting and at home?	✓	Records of learning and development	
A range of materials and experiences for the children?	✓	Planning	
Accessible resources and toys so children can make choices?	✓	Visit notes from Local Authority	

If you have ticked no to any question, use this as a basis to complete an action plan as on page 40 to identify what you need to find out more about and how to develop your practice or environment.

Communication and Language – Listening and attention

THE UNIQUENESS OF YOUR CHILDREN – How much do you know about the children in your key group?

Do you know....	Yes	Where is the evidence?	No
How each key child responds and reacts to interaction?			
What each key child enjoys exploring?			
What sounds each key child enjoys?			
What familiar words or songs each key child responds to?			

POSITIVE RELATIONSHIPS – What do you do?

Do you....	Yes	When or where?	No
Spend time being close with each key child?			
Play turn taking, playful games like peek-a-boo?			
Sing songs and rhymes during everyday routines?			
Use repeated words and phrases that the children like?			

ENABLING ENVIRONMENTS – Do you have?

Do you have.....	Yes	Where?	No
Opportunities for children to be near each other and 'chat'?			
Songs and rhymes from each child's culture and home life (maybe shared by parents)?			
Copies of the children's favourite stories?			
Times when you sing with the children and encourage them to join in?			
A sensory environment which encourages everyone to touch, smell, feel, listen, explore and talk?			

If you have ticked no to any question, use this as a basis to complete an action plan as on page 40 to identify what you need to find out more about and how to develop your practice or environment.

THE UNIQUENESS OF YOUR CHILDREN – How much do you know about the children in your key group?

Do you know....	Yes	Where is the evidence?	No
The stories and rhymes your key children know and enjoy?			
The sounds each child recognises e.g. the dinner trolley, the knock at the door?			
The stories each of your key children know and like to join in with?			
The activities and experiences each key child can concentrate on if s/he has chosen it?			

POSITIVE RELATIONSHIPS – What do you do?

Do you....	Yes	When or where?	No
Make different noises and sounds when you read stories?			
Play games where children can guess the object from the sound?			
Ensure you say all the children's names correctly?			
Remember to use the children's names first to get their attention?			
Talk about the different sounds the children might hear?			
Remember children may not appear to hear if busy playing?			

ENABLING ENVIRONMENTS – Do you have?

Do you have.....	Yes	Where?	No
Lots of different poems, rhymes and songs?			
Resources that makes different sounds?			
Background noise to a minimum?			
Sounds and music that are used for particular reasons e.g. calming down, tidy up, to dance to?			
Opportunities for children to learn each other's names?			
Poems, rhymes, songs and stories from the children's home backgrounds and cultures?			
Time when children can choose to listen to a story or not?			

If you have ticked no to any question, use this as a basis to complete an action plan as on page 40 to identify what you need to find out more about and how to develop your practice or environment.

The EYFS: Am I getting it right? © Anita Soni & Sue Bristow

THE UNIQUENESS OF YOUR CHILDREN – How much do you know about the children in your key group?			
Do you know....	Yes	*Where is the evidence?*	No
The stories each child loves listening to?			
Each child's favourite rhymes and songs?			
Who each child likes to talk to and play with?			
The type of activities each child can concentrate on and be focused?			

POSITIVE RELATIONSHIPS – What do you do?			
Do you....	Yes	*When or where?*	No
Listen to what the children tell you with attention and respect?			
Cue children in to what you are going to be talking about?			
Use children's names before giving an instruction?			
Share stories, rhymes and books from other cultures?			
Do you sometimes use languages other than English?			
Play games where children have to listen e.g. Simon Say?			
Listen to the different sounds that can be heard at different times, inside or out?			
Explain why it is important to listen to each other?			

ENABLING ENVIRONMENTS – Do you have?			
Do you have.....	Yes	*Where?*	No
Song or rhyme bags for children to take home and sing or read with their parents?			
Times where children speak and listen to each other?			
Ideas for games that draw attention to words and names that start with the same sound?			
Listening games where children have to listen carefully e.g. whisper a sound round a group?			
Times where children can make up their own rhymes to the last word in a nursery rhyme?			
A listening area where children can listen to songs and rhymes?			
Stories with repetition such as Going on a Bear Hunt?			
Songs with actions, replies and turn taking e.g. Tommy Thumb?			
Times where children can listen to each other sing or tell a story?			
Sand timers to help children extend concentration?			

If you have ticked no to any question, use this as a basis to complete an action plan as on page 40 to identify what you need to find out more about and how to develop your practice or environment.

THE UNIQUENESS OF YOUR CHILDREN – How much do you know about the children in your key group?

Do you know....	Yes	Where is the evidence?	No
The sounds and gestures each child recognises?			
The words and phrases each child understands?			
How each child responds to familiar things said by a special person?			

POSITIVE RELATIONSHIPS – What do you do?

Do you....	Yes	When or where?	No
Make eye contact when talking to each child?			
Talk and give meaning to what a child shows an interest in?			
Talk about what you are doing with the children?			
Use actions alongside your words e.g. showing a plate at dinner time?			
Speak clearly to the children?			
Use and repeat single words at different times e.g. milk, snack to help children understand?			
Talk to parents about the words their child understands?			

ENABLING ENVIRONMENTS – Do you have?

Do you have.....	Yes	Where?	No
Predictable but flexible routines so children know what to expect?			
Resources that are stimulating for the children and their senses e.g. mirrors, soft cloth?			
Display words from the children's languages to show all are valued?			
Lists of words which involve parents displayed in the setting?			
Nursery rhymes and songs with actions as well as words?			

If you have ticked no to any question, use this as a basis to complete an action plan as on page 40 to identify what you need to find out more about and how to develop your practice or environment.

THE UNIQUENESS OF YOUR CHILDREN – How much do you know about the children in your key group?

Do you know....	Yes	Where is the evidence?	No
Which words each child understands?			
Which phrases or sentences each child understands?			
Which action words each child understands e.g. sitting?			
Which instructions each child can follow?			
Which question words e.g. who, what, each child understands?			

POSITIVE RELATIONSHIPS – What do you do?

Do you....	Yes	When or where?	No
Remember that children understand more than they can say?			
Appreciate and value when children understand new words or phrases?			
Use talk to explain what you are doing, or what the child is doing in their play or routines?			
Find out from parents what children understand at home?			

ENABLING ENVIRONMENTS – Do you have?

Do you have.....	Yes	Where?	No
Opportunities and spaces for children to talk to each other in pairs?			
Resources and activities for role play that children enjoy and understand e.g. pushchairs, changing bags?			
Pictures and objects to help children understand what is being said?			
Resources that are exciting and will help them want to communicate e.g. shells, hats, bubbles?			
Activities such as cooking or planting where talk is needed to plan?			
Times for children to talk to adults about what they see, hear, think and feel?			

If you have ticked no to any question, use this as a basis to complete an action plan as on page 40 to identify what you need to find out more about and how to develop your practice or environment.

THE UNIQUENESS OF YOUR CHILDREN – How much do you know about the children in your key group?

Do you know....	Yes	Where is the evidence?	No
The type of instruction each child understands?			
The prepositions such as in, on, under each child understands?			
Who can respond to other children or adult's talk and conversation?			
Who can understand how or why questions?			

POSITIVE RELATIONSHIPS – What do you do?

Do you....	Yes	When or where?	No
Get involved in children's play to prompt children's thinking and discussion?			
Encourage children to explain their ideas and talk about their play?			
Give clear instructions at the right level for the children?			
Reinforce understanding by using pictures or objects?			
Ask children to predict what they plan to do?			
Encourage children to talk about stories as they are being read?			
Talk to parents about the languages the child understands?			

ENABLING ENVIRONMENTS – Do you have?

Do you have.....	Yes	Where?	No
Stories where you can ask children to predict and guess what happens next?			
Stories which inspire children to talk about the characters, or the setting?			
Stories where children can explain what may have happened?			
Displays and photographs of experiences and activities the children have done to encourage talk?			
Role play and story telling props so children can re-enact familiar events and stories?			
Practical experiences that encourage the children to question and talk?			
Resources for imaginative and role play so children can act out events from real life or their imaginations?			

If you have ticked no to any question, use this as a basis to complete an action plan as on page 40 to identify what you need to find out more about and how to develop your practice or environment.

THE UNIQUENESS OF YOUR CHILDREN – How much do you know about the children in your key group?

Do you know....	Yes	Where is the evidence?	No
How each child communicates their needs and feelings?			
How each child responds to others?			
The sounds and noises or words each child uses?			
How each child shows they are interested or wants something?			
The special words each child uses at home or at the setting?			

POSITIVE RELATIONSHIPS – What do you do?

Do you....	Yes	When or where?	No
Know the languages spoken in the homes of the children?			
Talk to parents about the value of their home language?			
Copy and turn take in conversations with each child?			
Talk to parents about the words each child uses at the setting or at home?			
Respond to children talk and early attempts to do so?			
Say words clearly after a child has said it so the child can hear the name clearly?			
Use children, parent and staff's home languages in the setting at different times e.g. greeting, meal times?			

ENABLING ENVIRONMENTS – Do you have?

Do you have.....	Yes	Where?	No
Key words in the home language of each child?			
Recorders for parents to record familiar sounds and songs for children?			
Lists of children's words for items that are special to them such as soothers, and cups?			
Show and value the languages spoken by staff, children and parents?			

If you have ticked no to any question, use this as a basis to complete an action plan as on page 40 to identify what you need to find out more about and how to develop your practice or environment.

THE UNIQUENESS OF YOUR CHILDREN – How much do you know about the children in your key group?			
Do you know….	Yes	Where is the evidence?	No
The expressions e.g. oh no! that each child likes to copy?			
Examples of the words (nouns, verbs and adjectives) or phrases/sentences each child says?			
The types of questions each child asks?			
The people and events each child likes to talk about?			
Who each child likes to talk to?			
The languages the child speaks at home?			

POSITIVE RELATIONSHIPS – What do you do?			
Do you….	Yes	When or where?	No
Give choices to encourage children to speak?			
Develop children's language by repeating and adding another word to their phrases or sentences?			
Repeat words correctly that children pronounce incorrectly rather than telling the child they got it wrong?			
Praise and encourage use of children's home language?			
Support and encourage children's communication e.g. gestures, signs?			
Follow children's lead in talk?			
Give children time to think before they respond?			
Introduce the children to new words?			

ENABLING ENVIRONMENTS – Do you have?			
Do you have…..	Yes	Where?	No
Time and space to follow children's ideas whilst using new words?			
Stories with repetitive phrases to read aloud to children to develop their vocabulary or language structures?			
Displays or books of photographs of familiar activities or events to talk about?			
Activities that encourage children to hear patterns and differences in rhymes, rhythms and words?			
A wide range of interesting play activities and experiences to extend children's vocabulary?			
Opportunities for children to speak in their language if other than English?			

If you have ticked no to any question, use this as a basis to complete an action plan as on page 40 to identify what you need to find out more about and how to develop your practice or environment.

THE UNIQUENESS OF YOUR CHILDREN – How much do you know about the children in your key group?			
Do you know....	Yes	Where is the evidence?	No
The types of sentences each child says?			
Who can talk about an event in the correct sequence?			
The types of questions each child asks?			
The verb tenses each child uses e.g. sleep, slept, will sleep?			
The interesting words each child uses?			
The language used in role play and imaginative play?			
Who uses a story line in their play?			
Who connects ideas and events together in their talk?			

POSITIVE RELATIONSHIPS – What do you do?			
Do you....	Yes	When or where?	No
Use open questions where a range of answers is possible?			
Use more statements more questions?			
Show an interest in what children say ?			
Expand on what children say by introducing new words or using more complex sentences?			
Value all children's communication e.g. in sign, home language or gesture, and contributions?			
Give children thinking time before expecting an answer?			
Encourage turn taking and conversation between children?			
Model how to use language in different situations e.g. to negotiate, for a visitor?			
Encourage language play e.g. nonsense songs and stories?			

ENABLING ENVIRONMENTS – Do you have?			
Do you have.....	Yes	Where?	No
A wide range of stimulating play activities and experiences to extend children's vocabulary?			
Opportunities for children who speak English as an Additional Language time to speak their language?			
Time for children to initiate talk and discussion?			
Collaborative opportunities where children will talk together and play e.g. role play?			
Opportunities for the children to think about and use key vocabulary for new experiences?			
Opportunities for the children to talk for different reasons e.g. to share news, to think up an activity?			
Opportunities for children to talk and share with each other e.g. talk about what may happen next in the story?			

If you have ticked no to any question, use this as a basis to complete an action plan as on page 40 to identify what you need to find out more about and how to develop your practice or environment.

THE UNIQUENESS OF YOUR CHILDREN – How much do you know about the children in your key group?

Do you know....	Yes	Where is the evidence?	No
The movements each child can make e.g. rolling, lifting head?			
How each child explores using his/her hands, feet and mouth?			
Which key children can sit (supported or unsupported)?			
Who can pull to stand?			
How each mobile child prefers to move?			

POSITIVE RELATIONSHIPS – What do you do?

Do you....	Yes	When or where?	No
Help children to be aware of their bodies through touch and movement?			
Offer toys to squeeze, grasp and hold?			
Encourage control of the bottle gradually?			
Encourage children to notice other children moving near them?			
Support children's drive to stand or move?			
Remember children have little sense of danger?			
Play finger games e.g. round and round the garden?			

ENABLING ENVIRONMENTS – Do you have?

Do you have.....	Yes	Where?	No
Access to varied physical experiences e.g. bouncing, rocking indoor and outdoors?			
Objects that children can hold, throw and squeeze?			
Gloop, dough and paint for children to make marks in?			
Interesting materials for children to move on and explore?			
Space for children to stretch and move?			
Low level equipment for children to use to pull up on or walk between?			
Tunnels, small steps and slopes for mobile children?			
Push along and trundle toys for indoors and outdoors?			
Accessible toys for children to reach and fetch?			
Resources that stimulate use of fingers and hands e.g. buttons to press, flaps to lift?			

If you have ticked no to any question, use this as a basis to complete an action plan as on page 40 to identify what you need to find out more about and how to develop your practice or environment.

The EYFS: Am I getting it right? © Anita Soni & Sue Bristow

THE UNIQUENESS OF YOUR CHILDREN – How much do you know about the children in your key group?

Do you know….	Yes	Where is the evidence?	No
How each child manages going up and down stairs?			
How each child can balance bricks in a tower?			
How each child walks or runs?			
How well each child can climb on ladders and steps?			
How each child's fine motor skills are e.g. in picking up small items, or turning pages, holding a pencil, pouring drinks?			
How each child can kick or throw a ball?			

POSITIVE RELATIONSHIPS – What do you do?

Do you….	Yes	When or where?	No
Encourage independence in dressing, eating and drinking?			
Encourage children to have periods of activity and calmness?			
Explore and talk to the children about different ways of moving?			
Encourage children to be safe but allow them to explore?			
Support children in using their fine motor skills in play?			

ENABLING ENVIRONMENTS – Do you have?

Do you have…..	Yes	Where?	No
Stories that talk about different ways of moving?			
Utensils to help children eat and drink independently?			
As much choice as possible for children to be indoors or outdoors?			
Safe spaces for children to move and play in?			
Music and equipment to encourage rhythmic movement?			
Resources to encourage different ways of moving such as rolling and crawling?			
Wheeled toys indoors and outdoors?			
Resources to fill, empty and carry things in?			
Resources so children can help with daily routines?			
Sticks rollers and other resources for clay, dough and sand?			
Different surfaces and levels to play on?			
Large flexible play equipment?			
Activities that encourage moving and stopping?			
Tool boxes of mark making equipment in and outdoors?			

If you have ticked no to any question, use this as a basis to complete an action plan as on page 40 to identify what you need to find out more about and how to develop your practice or environment.

THE UNIQUENESS OF YOUR CHILDREN – How much do you know about the children in your key group?

Do you know....	Yes	Where is the evidence?	No
The different ways each child can move in?			
How each child climbs and balances on equipment or stairs?			
How well each child can jump or stand on one leg?			
How each child can throw, catch or kick balls?			
How well each child can manipulate one handed tools?			
How each child holds and controls a pencil?			
How much control each child has with malleable materials?			
How well each child can move around obstacles in a space?			

POSITIVE RELATIONSHIPS – What do you do?

Do you....	Yes	When or where?	No
Use varied vocabulary to describe movement and manipulation?			
Use music to encourage different moods and movement?			
Encourage children to be active in games?			
Help the children understand safety rules?			
Give children challenges to move in different ways or with control?			
Encourage children to play ball games with each other when their skills are sufficient?			
Teach and then let children use tools and materials safely?			

ENABLING ENVIRONMENTS – Do you have?

Do you have.....	Yes	Where?	No
Sensible rules to follow in using equipment and movement?			
Time and space for daily energetic play?			
Large portable equipment so children can create large structures e.g. milk crate, tubes, tyres?			
Beanbags, cones, balls and hoops to practice movement skills?			
Activities where children can move in different ways and speeds?			
Activities where children can balance and throw, roll, kick & catch?			
Sufficient equipment for children not to have to wait too long?			
Marked out areas for different types of physical play?			
Activities for manipulative skills e.g. clay , small world, threading, posting toys, dolls' clothes, collage material, paint and cooking?			
A range of construction toys of different sizes and materials that fit together in different ways?			
Left handed resources for children that need them?			

If you have ticked no to any question, use this as a basis to complete an action plan as on page 40 to identify what you need to find out more about and how to develop your practice or environment.

THE UNIQUENESS OF YOUR CHILDREN – How much do you know about the children in your key group?

Do you know....	Yes	Where is the evidence?	No
How each child expresses discomfort, hunger or thirst?			
Who can hold their own bottle or cup?			
The stage of self feeding each child is at e.g. with a spoon, finger feeding?			
How each child responds to nappy changing?			
How each child cues that s/he is ready to engage?			

POSITIVE RELATIONSHIPS – What do you do?

Do you....	Yes	When or where?	No
Encourage children to gradually share control of food and drink?			
Talk to parents about feeding patterns and care of skin and hair?			
Talk to children when you hold them or are with them to show they are secure and safe?			
Talk to parents about how their child communicates his/her needs?			
Encourage enjoyment of healthy food?			
Remember children have little sense of danger at this age?			

ENABLING ENVIRONMENTS – Do you have?

Do you have.....	Yes	Where?	No
A record of the individual cultural and feeding needs of each child?			
An awareness of any specific health needs of each child?			
A comfortable, accessible place where children can rest or sleep when they want?			
Alternative activities for children who do not want to rest or sleep?			
Mealtime seating where young children can have their feet on the floor or a rest as this aids hand to mouth co-ordination?			
Safe surroundings where children have the freedom to move but are kept safe by watchful adults?			

If you have ticked no to any question, use this as a basis to complete an action plan as on page 40 to identify what you need to find out more about and how to develop your practice or environment.

Physical Development – Health and Self-care

Physical Development – Health and Self-care

THE UNIQUENESS OF YOUR CHILDREN – How much do you know about the children in your key group?			
Do you know....	Yes	Where is the evidence?	No
What each child likes and dislikes in food and drink?			
The type of cup each child can drink from independently?			
The stage of toileting each child is at e.g. in nappies and says if wet or soiled, bowel and bladder urges, asking for potty or toilet?			
How each child likes to be taken to the toilet or changed?			
How each child can eat independently?			
The dressing and undressing skills of each child?			

POSITIVE RELATIONSHIPS – What do you do?			
Do you....	Yes	When or where?	No
Encourage children to try new tastes and textures?			
Encourage children in dressing and undressing independently alongside with family expectations?			
Talk to parents about expectations of independence?			
Respond quickly and appropriately when a child communicates hunger, thirst or for the toilet?			
Work in partnership with parents in toileting?			
Involve children in preparing food?			
Talk about food choices and encourage healthy foods?			
Have a respect for different ways of eating e.g. fingers?			

ENABLING ENVIRONMENTS – Do you have?			
Do you have.....	Yes	Where?	No
Resources and time for children to do things for themselves such as pour drinks, putting on own shoes?			
Routines where children can help themselves e.g. aprons?			
Time to discuss healthy choices of food or drinks?			
Accessible cups and water for children to get a drink as needed?			
Choices for children for toileting e.g. step, potty, trainer seat?			
Opportunities for children to make choices?			
Stories that show consequences of different choices?			
Colourful daily menu showing meals and snacks for children and parents?			
A balance between safety and allowing risk taking?			

If you have ticked no to any question, use this as a basis to complete an action plan as on page 40 to identify what you need to find out more about and how to develop your practice or environment.

THE UNIQUENESS OF YOUR CHILDREN – How much do you know about the children in your key group?			
Do you know....	Yes	*Where is the evidence?*	No
Who will say if they are hungry, thirsty or tired?			
The toileting needs of each child?			
How much support each child needs in terms of hygiene e.g. reminders to wash hands?			
How much help each child needs with dressing?			
The different types of food or drink each child will have?			
How much understanding each child has of safety?			

POSITIVE RELATIONSHIPS – What do you do?			
Do you....	Yes	*When or where?*	No
Explain why certain things are needed e.g. rest or coat on wet day?			
Help children notice changes in their body from exercise?			
Help children understand hygiene e.g. hand washing?			
Encourage and praise children for managing their own care as much as they can?			
Encourage the use and return of resources appropriately e.g. put gloves in their coat pocket?			
Talk to parents sensitively about healthy choices?			
Encourage children to self regulate e.g. the need for rest, a drink?			

ENABLING ENVIRONMENTS – Do you have?			
Do you have.....	Yes	*Where?*	No
A cosy area where children can rest quietly?			
Active experiences every day for all children?			
Lively, energetic games to help promote fun physical activity?			
Opportunities to talk to children about their bodies and how they change after activity or eating?			
A range of physical activities that interests the children and matches their abilities?			
A colourful menu showing what the children can choose to eat, and discuss the choices that could be made?			

If you have ticked no to any question, use this as a basis to complete an action plan as on page 40 to identify what you need to find out more about and how to develop your practice or environment.

Physical Development – Health and Self-care

THE UNIQUENESS OF YOUR CHILDREN – How much do you know about the children in your key group?

Do you know....	Yes	Where is the evidence?	No
How each child responds when they are interacted with?			
Who each child likes to be with best, children and adults, at the setting and at home?			
What each child likes to do?			
How each child responds to new people or situations?			

POSITIVE RELATIONSHIPS – What do you do?

Do you....	Yes	When or where?	No
Have a key person for each child who knows the child well and understands their needs and wants?			
Respond sensitively and quickly to each child's needs?			
Follow the child's lead in whether they want interaction or to be left alone?			
Ensure each child and parent are greeted personally on arrival and departure by staff or children?			

ENABLING ENVIRONMENTS – Do you have?

Do you have.....	Yes	Where?	No
Displays of photographs of the special people in each child's life at home and in the setting?			
A buddy for each key person who can step in as needed?			
Individual time with each child when they are alert and happy to engage?			
Knowledge about the languages the children hear and use at home?			
Routines for greetings at the start and end of each session to create daily rituals?			
Information from parents on what each child enjoys at home or elsewhere?			

If you have ticked no to any question, use this as a basis to complete an action plan as on page 40 to identify what you need to find out more about and how to develop your practice or environment.

THE UNIQUENESS OF YOUR CHILDREN – How much do you know about the children in your key group?			
Do you know....	Yes	*Where is the evidence?*	No
When and whether each child prefers to play alone and alongside other children?			
When each child is likely to worry and need support?			
What each child needs if they do get worried or upset?			
Who joins in with other children's play?			
How each child likes to show affection or concern for others?			
Who each child is forming special relationships with?			

POSITIVE RELATIONSHIPS – What do you do?			
Do you....	Yes	*When or where?*	No
Involve children in greeting and caring for each other?			
Give each child your full attention when they look for a response?			
Have a key person for each child?			
Talk about children's emotions e.g. happy, sad, angry?			
Let children choose to join in activities?			
Help children understand and recognise simple rules such as how to play together or wait for a go?			
Model responding to how other people may feel?			

ENABLING ENVIRONMENTS – Do you have?			
Do you have.....	Yes	*Where?*	No
Name games so children know each other's names and those of the staff?			
Time to reflect on how staff respond to different children?			
Opportunities for children to play alongside others or in simple cooperative games with an adult to support?			
Sufficient resources that adults and children can mimic each other in play e.g. same musical shaker?			
Time for children to be with their key person individually and in their key group?			
Cosy areas where children can sit and chat together?			
Resources that promote cooperation between two or three children e.g. big ball?			

If you have ticked no to any question, use this as a basis to complete an action plan as on page 40 to identify what you need to find out more about and how to develop your practice or environment.

Personal, social, emotional development – Making relationships

THE UNIQUENESS OF YOUR CHILDREN – How much do you know about the children in your key group?

Do you know....	Yes	Where is the evidence?	No
Who can play in a group with others and when this happens?			
Who initiates play with others and when this happens?			
Who can keep play going with others?			
Who is friendly with other children and adults and when this occurs?			
Who is able to compromise with others and when this occurs?			
Who each child has positive relationships with and when these are most likely to occur?			

POSITIVE RELATIONSHIPS – What do you do?

Do you....	Yes	When or where?	No
Support children to develop positive relationships with other children and adults?			
Challenge all negative comments and actions to others?			
Encourage children to play with a range of children from different backgrounds?			
Help children understand feelings of others by labelling emotions such as lonely, scared or worried?			
Plan and support children who have not yet made friends?			
Act as a role model, by responding considerately and sensitively to other children and adults?			
Ensure children and adults have opportunities to speak and listen to each other to explain their actions?			
Have an awareness of the needs of children with English as an Additional Language?			

ENABLING ENVIRONMENTS – Do you have?

Do you have.....	Yes	Where?	No
Collaborative opportunities for children e.g. ring games?			
Stability in the key person role and grouping of children?			
Time, space and resources for children to be together in different size groups?			
Role play resources that both reflect children's lives and unfamiliar items to broaden their interests?			
Books, puppets and dolls that explore feelings & friendships?			
Opportunities for children to know children beyond their special friends?			
Time for children to be with their key person alone or in a group?			
Turn taking and sharing opportunities in small groups?			

If you have ticked no to any question, use this as a basis to complete an action plan as on page 40 to identify what you need to find out more about and how to develop your practice or environment.

The EYFS: Am I getting it right? © Anita Soni & Sue Bristow

THE UNIQUENESS OF YOUR CHILDREN – How much do you know about the children in your key group?

Do you know....	Yes	Where is the evidence?	No
How each child gains the attention of others?			
The type of interaction and play each child likes?			
How each child gets other people to do things for him/her?			
Which parts of the body each child can point to?			

POSITIVE RELATIONSHIPS – What do you do?

Do you....	Yes	When or where?	No
Show you enjoy being with each child?			
Respond to each child's expression and action?			
Find out each child likes and dislikes from parents?			
Give the children opportunities to choose?			
Follow the children's lead as they explore?			
Talk to the children as you do things?			

ENABLING ENVIRONMENTS – Do you have?

Do you have.....	Yes	Where?	No
A sofa or comfy chairs for parents and practitioners to sit on with the children?			
Objects for children to hold during routines such as changing or eating?			
Times for the younger children to play with the older children?			
Uninterrupted time to play and talk to the children?			
Time to talk to parents regularly about their child?			
Mirrors so the children can see themselves?			
Choices for the children e.g. between snacks, toys and activities?			
Space for children to move and explore?			

If you have ticked no to any question, use this as a basis to complete an action plan as on page 40 to identify what you need to find out more about and how to develop your practice or environment.

Personal, social, emotional development – Self-confidence and self-awareness

THE UNIQUENESS OF YOUR CHILDREN – How much do you know about the children in your key group?

Do you know....	Yes	Where is the evidence?	No
When each child is likely to need to check in for security?			
What type of pretend play each child enjoys?			
The things each child likes to do independently?			
Each child's preferences and interests?			

POSITIVE RELATIONSHIPS – What do you do?

Do you....	Yes	When or where?	No
Model and join in pretend play?			
Have secure key person relationships with your key children?			
Encourage and support the children to try to do things independently?			
Respond to children's changing interests and preferences?			
Talk to children about choices they make?			
Know when each child may need more support?			
Recognise each child's efforts e.g. by high fives or praise?			

ENABLING ENVIRONMENTS – Do you have?

Do you have.....	Yes	Where?	No
Ways children can express their choices e.g. for toys, activities, snacks?			
Photographs of the key people (staff) accessible to the children and parents?			
Photographs of children playing to support talk about activities?			
Time to talk with parents and each other about how each child responds to activities, adults and other children?			
Records of each child's achievements and progress at the setting and at home?			
A range of materials and experiences for the children?			
Accessible resources and toys so children can make choices?			

If you have ticked no to any question, use this as a basis to complete an action plan as on page 40 to identify what you need to find out more about and how to develop your practice or environment.

THE UNIQUENESS OF YOUR CHILDREN – How much do you know about the children in your key group?

Do you know….	Yes	Where is the evidence?	No
Who can choose what to play with and get what is needed?			
How each key child prefers to be praised?			
How confident each key child is with new adults or new situations?			
What each child is confident to talk about in front of others?			
Which activities each child is confident with?			
How each key child describes him or herself?			

POSITIVE RELATIONSHIPS – What do you do?

Do you….	Yes	When or where?	No
Have small tasks that children can do as helpers?			
Encourage children to play independently when they wish to and seek help from adults when they need it?			
Help children know what they are good at and describe themselves positively?			
Teach the children how to look after the resources?			
Value children's ideas and ways of doing things?			
Offer help sensitively when asked?			
Recognise and celebrate children's achievements for themselves?			
Support children to feel good about their own success rather than rely on a judgement from you?			

ENABLING ENVIRONMENTS – Do you have?

Do you have…..	Yes	Where?	No
Resources that the children can access and put away independently?			
Varied activities and experiences for the children?			
Records of children's achievements and progress?			
Time for children to pursue their ideas and interests over time e.g. to return to after dinner or on another day?			
Challenging and achievable experiences and activities?			
Opportunities for children to share their successes and achievements e.g. photographs or talk?			
Opportunities for children to talk to a small group about what they like or are interested in?			
Opportunities for children to record their opinions and preferences through photographs, talk or drawing?			

If you have ticked no to any question, use this as a basis to complete an action plan as on page 40 to identify what you need to find out more about and how to develop your practice or environment.

Personal, social, emotional development – Self-confidence and self-awareness

THE UNIQUENESS OF YOUR CHILDREN – How much do you know about the children in your key group?

Do you know....	Yes	Where is the evidence?	No
How each child prefers to be comforted?			
How each child shows pleasure, fear and excitement?			
When and how each child is likely to be anxious?			
How each child soothes him or herself e.g. with a comfort object?			
Which boundaries or phrases each child understands e.g. yes, no and stop?			

POSITIVE RELATIONSHIPS – What do you do?

Do you....	Yes	When or where?	No
Find out from parents, routines, how to settle and ways of communicating with each key child?			
Use calming processes such as rocking?			
Talk to parents about the ways they respond to their child?			
Have secure, warm relationships between each adult and their key children?			
Reassure key children at times that might be challenging e.g. when they leave their parents?			
Have clear, consistent boundaries for the children?			

ENABLING ENVIRONMENTS – Do you have?

Do you have.....	Yes	Where?	No
Familiar lullabies and songs that children know from home?			
Cosy, quiet places for children to be calm in?			
Comfortable seating for children to sit with their key person?			
Accessible toys and comfort items from home that children are familiar with e.g. teddy bears?			
Books and photographs that show different emotions?			
Opportunities to talk with parents about the boundaries at home and in the setting to create consistency?			

If you have ticked no to any question, use this as a basis to complete an action plan as on page 40 to identify what you need to find out more about and how to develop your practice or environment.

THE UNIQUENESS OF YOUR CHILDREN – How much do you know about the children in your key group?			
Do you know....	Yes	Where is the evidence?	No
How each child responds to other children's feelings?			
When each child may express strong feelings such as tantrums?			
Which boundaries each child knows and maintains?			
Which items children can share or find difficult to share?			
How each child expresses emotions?			
How each child responds to other children and adults?			

POSITIVE RELATIONSHIPS – What do you do?			
Do you....	Yes	When or where?	No
Talk to children about how they feel to develop emotional language?			
Balance the children's need to explore against possible risks and need for safety?			
Have flexible routines so children can pursue their own interests?			
Support children's symbolic play where they can try out different roles and feelings?			
Talk to children about ways to play with others?			
Help children to recognise when their actions hurt others and how to respond appropriately?			

ENABLING ENVIRONMENTS – Do you have?			
Do you have.....	Yes	Where?	No
Books and stories where characters help each other?			
Sufficient duplicates of resources to reduce conflict?			
An agreed behaviour policy and procedure that all staff understand and follow?			
A shared behaviour policy and procedure with parents?			
Areas where children can rest and relax?			
Spaces for children to be energetic and active?			
Books, stories and puppets to explore different feelings?			
Boundaries and routines that children understand and follow?			

If you have ticked no to any question, use this as a basis to complete an action plan as on page 40 to identify what you need to find out more about and how to develop your practice or environment.

Personal, social, emotional development – Managing feelings and behaviour

THE UNIQUENESS OF YOUR CHILDREN – How much do you know about the children in your key group?

Do you know....	Yes	Where is the evidence?	No
When each child can accept the needs of others, take turns or share?			
When each child can cope with frustration e.g. short delays?			
Who can adapt their behaviour to different situations and changes in routine?			
When each child recognises other children's feelings e.g. by helping or comforting another child?			
How each child may try and sort out a problem with another child?			

POSITIVE RELATIONSHIPS – What do you do?

Do you....	Yes	When or where?	No
Talk about different feelings such as anger, sadness, loneliness and happiness openly?			
Talk to children about ways of helping others feel better?			
Role model concern & care for others and the environment?			
Prepare the children for changes in the routine?			
Involve children in working out answers to problems?			
Role model being fair and talk about fairness?			
Praise and encourage positive behaviour?			
Help children think about other's views?			
Take time to listen to the children's views and concerns?			

ENABLING ENVIRONMENTS – Do you have?

Do you have.....	Yes	Where?	No
Clear behavioural expectations that the children and parents understand and respect?			
Clear rules that the children have created for their setting?			
Photographs and pictures of emotions?			
Music to inspire different emotions?			
Puppets and dolls to help understand different views?			
Ways children can express how they are feeling?			
Familiar predictable but flexible routines?			
Safe spaces for children to calm or be quiet?			
Small circle times to talk about different feelings?			
Activities and experiences that promote turn taking?			
Books and stories that show how one character's behaviour affects others?			

If you have ticked no to any question, use this as a basis to complete an action plan as on page 40 to identify what you need to find out more about and how to develop your practice or environment.

THE UNIQUENESS OF YOUR CHILDREN – How much do you know about the children in your key group?

Do you know….	Yes	Where is the evidence?	No
What books or printed material each child likes?			
Who each child likes to look at books or printed material with?			

POSITIVE RELATIONSHIPS – What do you do?

Do you….	Yes	When or where?	No
Know which rhymes and songs are sung at home with each child?			
Anticipate and allow space for children to respond to finger and word rhymes?			
Sing songs and rhymes that children know from home?			
Allow the children to handle the books and look at the pictures with them?			
Tell stories from memory so you can interact with the children?			

ENABLING ENVIRONMENTS – Do you have?

Do you have…..	Yes	Where?	No
A range of board books, cloth books and stories for the children?			
Family books with photographs of people from the children's lives at home?			
Photograph books showing everyday familiar objects?			
Photograph books showing familiar people from the setting?			

If you have ticked no to any question, use this as a basis to complete an action plan as on page 40 to identify what you need to find out more about and how to develop your practice or environment.

Literacy – Reading

THE UNIQUENESS OF YOUR CHILDREN – How much do you know about the children in your key group?

Do you know....	Yes	Where is the evidence?	No
Which books and stories each child likes?			
Which rhymes and songs each child likes?			
Who can fill in missing words in familiar rhymes or songs?			

POSITIVE RELATIONSHIPS – What do you do?

Do you....	Yes	When or where?	No
Encourage children to respond to the books and stories that are read to them?			
Use different voices to tell stories?			
Encourage the children to join in telling or reading the story?			
Encourage children to make links to stories in their play?			
Read stories children know and encourage them to 'read' the next bit?			

ENABLING ENVIRONMENTS – Do you have?

Do you have.....	Yes	Where?	No
CDs of rhymes, stories, sounds and songs?			
A range of picture books, books with flaps, books with accompanying CDs and story sacks for children to use?			
Story sacks and books for parents to borrow and use at home with their children?			
An attractive book area where children and adults can read together?			
Opportunities to tell or read stories to children using puppets, props or objects as props?			
Stories, pictures and puppets where children can talk about how the characters feel?			

If you have ticked no to any question, use this as a basis to complete an action plan as on page 40 to identify what you need to find out more about and how to develop your practice or environment.

Literacy – Reading

THE UNIQUENESS OF YOUR CHILDREN – How much do you know about the children in your key group?

Do you know....	Yes	Where is the evidence?	No
Which stories, rhymes and poems each child will join in with individually or in a group?			
Who is aware of how stories are structured e.g. where it happens, the main characters?			
Who will predict an ending to a story?			
The stories each child will listen to with attention and recall?			
Who is interested in print in the environment e.g. name, logos?			
The books each child enjoys and likes?			
How each child handles books e.g. carefully, correct way up?			
Who knows how English print works in books?			
Who knows sounds in words e.g. at the beginning?			
The words and sentences that each child can read or recall?			

POSITIVE RELATIONSHIPS – What do you do?

Do you....	Yes	When or where?	No
Look at similarities and differences between letters and words e.g. names, on food packets?			
Point out what a word is?			
Raise awareness of other language scripts?			
Talk about the characters in stories?			
Encourage children to predict endings for stories?			
Use non-fiction books to find things out?			
Encourage children to read or recall words they recognise e.g. names?			
Model blending and segmenting of letters in words if children are interested?			

ENABLING ENVIRONMENTS – Do you have?

Do you have.....	Yes	Where?	No
Home language or bilingual story sessions?			
Story sacks and boxes for children in the setting and to borrow for home use?			
Games of letter bingo for children to play if interested?			
Simple poetry, song, fiction and non-fiction books in different parts of the setting?			
Photograph books of familiar people and other texts e.g. catalogues that children can 'read'?			
Child-made and adult-scribed books in the book area?			
An environment with different types of print displayed?			
Written materials to show how reading is used e.g. recipe card?			
Visual cues and story props to go alongside stories and books?			
Opportunities to enact stories?			

If you have ticked no to any question, use this as a basis to complete an action plan as on page 40 to identify what you need to find out more about and how to develop your practice or environment.

THE UNIQUENESS OF YOUR CHILDREN – How much do you know about the children in your key group?

Do you know....	Yes	Where is the evidence?	No
How each child explores using his/her hands or feet?			
Who and where each child enjoys the sensory experience of making marks e.g. in sand, paint?			
The marks a child will make if holding a pen or crayon if interested?			
How each child communicates his/ her needs?			
The words and phrases each child understands?			

See Communication and Language Birth to 20 months for further questions.

POSITIVE RELATIONSHIPS – What do you do?

Do you....	Yes	When or where?	No
Talk about what you are doing with the children?			
Make eye contact and speak clearly to the children?			
Respond to children's communication?			
Listen, turn take and respond in 'chats' with each child?			
Talk and give meaning to what a child shows an interest in?			
Know the special words and home languages of each child?			

See Communication and Language Birth to 20 months for further questions.

ENABLING ENVIRONMENTS – Do you have?

Do you have.....	Yes	Where?	No
A stimulating environment which encourages exploration and communication?			
Special areas where children can be encouraged to talk to you and the other children?			
Rhymes, songs and stories that the children enjoy and are familiar with?			
First hand experiences and challenges that are appropriate to the development of the children?			

See Communication and Language Birth to 20 months for further questions.

If you have ticked no to any question, use this as a basis to complete an action plan as on page 40 to identify what you need to find out more about and how to develop your practice or environment.

The EYFS: Am I getting it right? © Anita Soni & Sue Bristow

THE UNIQUENESS OF YOUR CHILDREN – How much do you know about the children in your key group?

Do you know....	Yes	Where is the evidence?	No
Who can distinguish between the different marks they make?			
Who enjoys making marks?			
The sensory experiences each child prefers?			
The materials each child prefers to use?			

See Communication and Language 16 to 36 months for further questions.

POSITIVE RELATIONSHIPS – What do you do?

Do you....	Yes	When or where?	No
Listen and support what each child tells you about their marks?			
Draw the children's attention to marks, signs and symbols in the environment?			
Encourage children who are interested to mark make?			

See Communication and Language 16 to 36 months for further questions.

ENABLING ENVIRONMENTS – Do you have?

Do you have.....	Yes	Where?	No
Different signs, marks and symbols available in the environment to talk to children about?			
Representations of different types of marks and writing in the environment e.g. English writing, Hindi writing?			
Displays or books of photographs of familiar activities or events with writing in to talk about?			
Exciting resources to encourage children to communicate?			
Times for adults and children to talk together?			

See Communication and Language 16 to 36 months for further questions.

If you have ticked no to any question, use this as a basis to complete an action plan as on page 40 to identify what you need to find out more about and how to develop your practice or environment.

Literacy – Writing

THE UNIQUENESS OF YOUR CHILDREN – How much do you know about the children in your key group?

Do you know....	Yes	Where is the evidence?	No
Who gives meaning to their drawings?			
Who tries to give meaning to print they see in different places e.g. Cbeebies?			
Who can continue a rhyming string?			
Who can hear sounds in words e.g. at the beginning?			
How each child chooses to represent his/her name in writing?			
How each child attempts to do their own writing?			

POSITIVE RELATIONSHIPS – What do you do?

Do you....	Yes	When or where?	No
Respond when children show their early writing and marks?			
Support children to recognise and write their own name?			
Talk to children about letter sounds they are interested in?			
Write down things children say to support children's understanding of writing?			
Support and scaffold children's own writing attempts as the opportunities arise?			
Model writing different things e.g. lists or stories suggested by the children?			

ENABLING ENVIRONMENTS – Do you have?

Do you have.....	Yes	Where?	No
Books that you have made with the children with photographs as illustrations?			
Activities that may support children to experiment in writing e.g. message boxes			
Opportunities for writing in role play and other play?			
Word banks and writing resources to support indoor and outdoor play?			
Writing visible and appropriate in role play to show purposes of writing?			
Fun games and activities to encourage rhyming?			

If you have ticked no to any question, use this as a basis to complete an action plan as on page 40 to identify what you need to find out more about and how to develop your practice or environment.

THE UNIQUENESS OF YOUR CHILDREN – How much do you know about the children in your key group?			
Do you know....	Yes	Where is the evidence?	No
Who notices changes in the number of objects, images or sounds up to 3?			
How much each child is aware of numbers and number names?			
Who understands that things exist, even when out of sight?			

POSITIVE RELATIONSHIPS – What do you do?			
Do you....	Yes	When or where?	No
Sing number rhymes e.g. One, Two, Buckle My Shoe'?			
Move with each child to the rhythm patterns in familiar songs and rhymes?			
Encourage each child to join in with simple rhythms?			

ENABLING ENVIRONMENTS – Do you have?			
Do you have.....	Yes	Where?	No
Displays of favourite things where the children can see them?			
Groups of the same objects in treasure baskets, as well as single items, e.g. two fir cones or three shells?			
Mobiles where the number of items on it can be changed?			
A collection of repetitive number rhymes related to children's experiences, e.g. 'Peter Hammers with One Hammer'?			
Songs and rhymes used during personal routines e.g. 'Two Little Eyes to Look Around' pointing to their eyes one by one?			
A collection of number and counting rhymes from a range of cultures and in other languages?			

If you have ticked no to any question, use this as a basis to complete an action plan as on page 40 to identify what you need to find out more about and how to develop your practice or environment.

THE UNIQUENESS OF YOUR CHILDREN – How much do you know about the children in your key group?

Do you know....	Yes	Where is the evidence?	No
Who can organise and categorise objects, e.g. putting all the teddy bears together?			
The counting words each child uses?			
The number of objects each child can give when asked e.g. please give me one?			
Which number names each child can recite in sequence?			
How each child represents numbers with symbols and marks?			
When the children compare quantities?			
Who uses the language of quantities e.g. 'more', 'a lot'?			
Who knows that a group of things changes in quantity when something is added or taken away?			

POSITIVE RELATIONSHIPS – What do you do?

Do you....	Yes	When or where?	No
Use number words and maths meaningfully in everyday situations, e.g. 'Here is the other mitten. Now there's two'?			
Talk to children about 'lots' and 'few' as they play?			
Talk about children's choices demonstrating how counting helps us to find out how many?			
Talk to parents about all the ways children learn about numbers in your setting?			
Encourage parents of children learning English as an additional language to talk in their home language about quantities and numbers?			
Sing counting songs and rhymes such as 'Two Little Dickie Birds'?			
Play games relating to number order, addition and subtraction, e.g. hopscotch, skittles and target games?			

ENABLING ENVIRONMENTS – Do you have?

Do you have.....	Yes	Where?	No
Varied opportunities to explore 'lots' and 'few' in play?			
A role play area where things can be sorted in different ways?			
Collections of objects for sorting and matching?			
Resources that support children in making one to one correspondences e.g. giving each dolly a cup?			
A display made with the children about their favourite things to discuss how many like x or y e.g. apples or oranges?			
Props for children to act out counting songs and rhymes?			
Games and equipment that give opportunities for counting?			
A mathematical component in areas such as the sand, water or other play areas?			

If you have ticked no to any question, use this as a basis to complete an action plan as on page 40 to identify what you need to find out more about and how to develop your practice or environment.

Mathematics – Number

THE UNIQUENESS OF YOUR CHILDREN – How much do you know about the children in your key group?			
Do you know....	Yes	Where is the evidence?	No
The number names and number language used spontaneously by each child?			
The number names used accurately in play by each child?			
Who can recite numbers in order to 10?			
Who can identify how many objects are in a set?			
How each child represent numbers e.g. using fingers, marks on paper or pictures?			
Who sometimes matches numeral and quantity correctly?			
Who shows curiosity about numbers by offering comments or asking questions?			
Who compares two groups of objects, saying when they have the same number?			
Who shows an interest in number problems?			
Who separates a group of three or four objects in different ways, is beginning to recognise that the total is still the same?			
Who shows an interest in numerals in the environment?			
Who shows an interest in representing numbers?			
Who understands that anything can be counted, including steps, claps or jumps?			
The numerals of personal significance each child recognises?			
Who counts up to three or four objects by saying one number name for each item?			
Who counts actions or objects which cannot be moved?			
Who counts objects to 10, and is beginning to count to 10 +?			
Who counts out up to six objects from a larger group?			
Who select the correct numeral to represent 1 to 5, then 1 to 10 objects?			
Who can count an irregular arrangement of up to ten objects?			
Who can estimate how many objects they can see and checks by counting them?			
Who uses the language of 'more' and 'fewer' to compare sets of objects?			
Who can find the total number of items in two groups by counting them all of them?			
Who can say the number that is one more than a given number as well as when using objects of up to ten?			
Who is beginning to use the vocabulary involved in adding and subtracting, in practical activities and discussions?			
Who can record, using marks that they can interpret and explain?			
Who is beginning to identify own mathematical problems based on own interests and fascinations?			
Who can count reliably with numbers from one to 20?			
Who can place numbers one to 20 in order?			
Who can add and subtract two single-digit numbers and count on or back to find the answer?			
Who can solve problems, including doubling, halving and sharing?			

POSITIVE RELATIONSHIPS – What do you do?			
Do you....	Yes	When or where?	No
Use and encourage use of mathematical language in a variety of situations?			
Support children's understanding of abstraction by counting things that are not objects, such as hops, jumps?			
Model counting of objects in a random layout, showing the result is always the same as longs as each object is only counted once?			
Help the children to understand that one thing can be shared by number of pieces e.g. pizza?			

continued on next sheet

The EYFS: Am I getting it right? © Anita Soni & Sue Bristow

Mathematics – Number

Mathematics – Number

POSITIVE RELATIONSHIPS – What do you do? (continued)

Do you....	Yes	When or where?	No
As you read number stories or rhymes ask e.g. 'When one more frog jumps in, how many will there be in the pool altogether?'			
Use props to illustrate counting songs, rhymes etc.?			
Encourage children to use mark-making to support their thinking about numbers and simple problems?			
Talk with children about the strategies they are using to work out a simple problem by e.g. using fingers?			
Encourage estimation?			
Make books about numbers that have meaning for the child such as favourite numbers or birth dates?			
Use rhymes, songs and stories involving counting on and back in ones, twos, fives and tens?			
Emphasise the empty set and introduce the concept of nothing or zero?			
Make sure children are secure about the order of numbers before asking what comes after or before each number?			
Discuss with children how problems relate to others they have met, and their different solutions?			
Encourage children to make up their own story problems for other children to solve?			
Demonstrate methods of recording, using standard notation where appropriate?			
Give children learning English as an additional language opportunities to work in their home language to ensure accurate understanding of concepts?			

ENABLING ENVIRONMENTS – Do you have?

Do you have.....	Yes	Where?	No
Opportunities for children to count for a purpose?			
Opportunities for children to note the 'missing set'?			
Numerals displayed in purposeful context and provide number labels for children to use?			
Counting money and change in role-play games?			
Opportunities for children to separate objects into unequal groups as well as equal groups?			
Story props that children can use in their play?			
Collections of interesting things for children to sort, order, count and label in their play?			
Tactile numeral cards?			
Opportunities for children to experiment with a number of objects, the written numeral and the written number word?			
A 100 number square to show number patterns?			
Opportunities for children to count the things they see and talk about and use numbers beyond 10?			
Number games and number books?			
Opportunities for children to record what they have done e.g. tallying ?			
Number staircases and lines?			
Opportunities for children to be creative in identifying and devising problems and solutions?			
Opportunities children to understand that five fingers in each hand makes a total of ten altogether?			

If you have ticked no to any question, use this as a basis to complete an action plan as on page 40 to identify what you need to find out more about and how to develop your practice or environment.

The EYFS: Am I getting it right? © Anita Soni & Sue Bristow

THE UNIQUENESS OF YOUR CHILDREN – How much do you know about the children in your key group?			
Do you know....	Yes	Where is the evidence?	No
Who can recognise big and small things in meaningful contexts?			
Which parts of the daily routines, such as getting-up time, mealtimes, nappy time, bedtime, each child knows?			

See Physical Development Birth to 20 months for further questions.

POSITIVE RELATIONSHIPS – What do you do?			
Do you....	Yes	When or where?	No
Play games that involve curling, stretching, popping up and bobbing down?			
Encourage children's explorations of the characteristics of objects, e.g. by rolling a ball to them?			
Talk about what objects are like and how objects, such as a sponge, can change their shape by being squeezed or stretched?			

See Physical Development Birth to 20 months for further questions.

ENABLING ENVIRONMENTS – Do you have?			
Do you have.....	Yes	Where?	No
A range of objects of various textures and weights in treasure baskets?			
Books showing objects of different sizes such as a big truck and a little truck; or a big cat and a small kitten?			
Story props to support all children and particularly those learning English as an additional language?			

See Physical Development Birth to 20 months for further questions.

If you have ticked no to any question, use this as a basis to complete an action plan as on page 40 to identify what you need to find out more about and how to develop your practice or environment.

Mathematics – Shape, Space and Measures

THE UNIQUENESS OF YOUR CHILDREN – How much do you know about the children in your key group?

Do you know....	Yes	Where is the evidence?	No
The inset boards or jigsaw puzzles each child enjoys?			
The blocks used to create their own simple structures and arrangements?			
Who enjoys filling and emptying containers?			
Who knows the order of the daily routine and anticipates certain events like mealtimes?			
Who understands 'now', 'before', 'later' and 'soon'?			
When children notice simple shapes and patterns in pictures?			
Who can categorise objects according to shape or size?			
The language of size each child uses?			

POSITIVE RELATIONSHIPS – What do you do?

Do you....	Yes	When or where?	No
Use 'tidy up time' to promote reasoning about where things fit in or are kept?			
Talk to children about full, empty or containers holding more?			
Help children to create different arrangements of tracks?			
Help children to explore shape in art, music and dance?			
Talk about and help children to recognise patterns around them and in routines?			
Draw children's attention to the patterns and shapes in the environment?			
Use descriptive words like 'big' and 'little'?			
Use consistent vocabulary for weight and mass?			

ENABLING ENVIRONMENTS – Do you have?

Do you have.....	Yes	Where?	No
Opportunities where children are encouraged to sort e.g. put pieces of apple on one dish the pieces of celery on another?			
Pictures or shapes of objects to indicate where things are kept and encourage children to work out where things belong?			
Different sizes and shapes of containers in water play?			
A range of puzzles with large pieces and knobs or handles?			
Pictures that illustrate the use of shapes and patterns from a variety of cultures e.g. Arabic designs?			
Opportunities for children to measure time (sand timer) weight (balances) and length (rulers or string)?			
Different volume and capacity equipment in the sand/water?			
Opportunities to use coins and containers and bags for sorting?			

If you have ticked no to any question, use this as a basis to complete an action plan as on page 40 to identify what you need to find out more about and how to develop your practice or environment.

THE UNIQUENESS OF YOUR CHILDREN – How much do you know about the children in your key group?

Do you know....	Yes	Where is the evidence?	No
How each child likes to play with shape and space e.g. making arrangements with objects, construction?			
Who is aware of similarities of shapes in the environment?			
Who uses positional language and everyday language related to time and money?			
Who talks about shapes in the environment and of everyday objects e.g. 'round' and 'tall'?			
When each child uses shapes appropriately for tasks?			
The language used by each child to describe 'solid' 3D shapes and 'flat' shapes and properties of shapes?			
Who can find a particular named shape?			
The language used by each child to describe relative position e.g. 'behind' or 'next to'?			
Who can order two or three items by length or height?			
Who can order two items by weight or capacity?			
Who uses familiar objects and common shapes to create and recreate patterns and build models?			
Who can order and sequence familiar events?			
Who can measure short periods of time in simple ways?			

POSITIVE RELATIONSHIPS – What do you do?

Do you....	Yes	When or where?	No
Demonstrate the language for shape, position and measures including when using children's home language?			
Encourage children to talk about the shapes they see and use and how they are arranged and used in constructions?			
Value children's constructions?			
Ask 'silly' questions e.g. show a tiny box and ask if there is a bicycle in it?			
Play peek-a-boo, revealing shapes a little at a time and at different angles, asking children to say what they think the shape is, what else it could be or what it could not be?			
Be a robot and ask children to give you instructions to get to somewhere?			
Introduce children to the use of mathematical names for 'solid' 3D shapes and 'flat' 2D shapes, and the mathematical terms to describe shapes?			
Encourage children to use everyday words to describe position?			

ENABLING ENVIRONMENTS – Do you have?

Do you have.....	Yes	Where?	No
Opportunities in the environment to match irregular and regular shapes?			
Large and small blocks and boxes available for construction both indoors and outdoors?			
Opportunities to play games involving children positioning themselves?			
Rich and varied opportunities for comparing length, weight, capacity and time?			
Stories to read and talk about distance and stimulate discussion about non standard units and the need for standard units?			
Books about shape, time and measure made by the children?			
Areas where children can explore the properties of objects and where they can weigh and measure?			
Opportunities for children to describe and compare shapes, measures and distance?			
Materials and resources for children to observe symmetry and describe patterns in the indoor and outdoor environment and in daily routines?			

If you have ticked no to any question, use this as a basis to complete an action plan as on page 40 to identify what you need to find out more about and how to develop your practice or environment.

Mathematics – Shape, Space and Measures

THE UNIQUENESS OF YOUR CHILDREN – How much do you know about the children in your key group?

Do you know….	Yes	Where is the evidence?	No
How each child responds when they are interacted with?			
Who each child likes to be with best, children and adults, at the setting and at home?			
What each child likes to do?			
How each child responds to new people or situations?			
How each child responds to other children and adults?			
How each child responds to familiar things said by a special person?			

See Personal, Social and Emotional Development and Communication and Language Birth to 20 months for further questions.

POSITIVE RELATIONSHIPS – What do you do?

Do you….	Yes	When or where?	No
Find out each child likes and dislikes from parents?			
Do you sometimes use languages other than English?			

See Personal, Social and Emotional Development and Communication and Language Birth to 20 months for further questions.

ENABLING ENVIRONMENTS – Do you have?

Do you have…..	Yes	Where?	No
Information from parents on what each child enjoys at home or elsewhere?			
Displays of photographs of the special people in each child's life at home and in the setting?			
Opportunities to use children, parent and staff's home languages in the setting at different times e.g. greeting, meal times?			
Songs and rhymes from each child's culture and home life (maybe shared by parents)?			

See Personal, Social and Emotional Development and Communication and Language Birth to 20 months for further questions.

If you have ticked no to any question, use this as a basis to complete an action plan as on page 40 to identify what you need to find out more about and how to develop your practice or environment.

THE UNIQUENESS OF YOUR CHILDREN – How much do you know about the children in your key group?

Do you know....	Yes	Where is the evidence?	No
Who is curious about people and shows interest in stories about themselves and their family?			
Enjoys pictures and stories about themselves, their families and other people?			
Who has a sense of own immediate family and relations?			
Imitates everyday actions and events from own family and cultural background e.g. making and drinking tea?			
Who is beginning to have friends?			
Who understands that they have similarities and differences that connect them to, and distinguish them from, others?			

POSITIVE RELATIONSHIPS – What do you do?

Do you....	Yes	When or where?	No
Help children to learn each other's names?			
Be positive about differences between people and support children's acceptance of difference?			
Ensure that each child is recognised as a valuable contributor to the group?			
Celebrate and value cultural, religious and community events and experiences?			
Talk to children about their friends, their families, and why they are important?			

ENABLING ENVIRONMENTS – Do you have?

Do you have.....	Yes	Where?	No
Opportunities for babies to see people and things beyond the baby room, including the activities of older children			
Stories and make books about children in the group, showing things they like to do?			
Books and resources which represent children's diverse backgrounds and which avoid negative stereotypes?			
Photographic books about the children in the setting and encourage parents to contribute to these?			
Positive images of all children?			
Photographs of children's families, friends, friends, pets or favourite people?			
Opportunities to support children's understanding of difference and of empathy by using props to tell stories about diverse experiences, ensuring that negative stereotyping is avoided?			

If you have ticked no to any question, use this as a basis to complete an action plan as on page 40 to identify what you need to find out more about and how to develop your practice or environment.

Understanding the World – People and Communities

THE UNIQUENESS OF YOUR CHILDREN – How much do you know about the children in your key group?

Do you know....	Yes	Where is the evidence?	No
Who shows an interest in the lives of people who are familiar to them and talks about significant events in their own experience, past and present?			
Who shows an interest in different occupations and ways of life?			
Who knows some of the things that make them unique, and can talk about some of the similarities and differences in relation to friends or family?			
Who enjoy joining in with family customs and routines?			
Who knows that other children don't always enjoy the same things, and are sensitive to this?			
Who knows about similarities and differences between communities and traditions?			

POSITIVE RELATIONSHIPS – What do you do?

Do you....	Yes	When or where?	No
Encourage children to talk about their own home and community life, and to find out about other children's experiences, in their home language as well if appropriate?			
Encourage children to develop positive relationships with community members?			
Encourage children to share their feelings and talk about why they respond to experiences in particular ways?			
Explain carefully why some children may need extra help or support for some things, or why some children feel upset by a particular thing?			
Help children and parents to see the ways in which their cultures and beliefs are similar?			
Strengthen positive impressions children have their own cultures and faiths, and those of others in their community?			

ENABLING ENVIRONMENTS – Do you have?

Do you have.....	Yes	Where?	No
Activities and opportunities for children to share experiences and knowledge from different parts of their lives with each other?			
Ways of preserving memories of special events?			
Opportunities to invite children and families with experiences for living in other countries to bring photographs and objects from their home cultures?			
Modern photographs of parts of the world that are commonly stereotyped and misrepresented?			
Opportunities for the children to learn positive attitudes and challenge negative attitudes and stereotypes?			
Opportunities to visit different parts of the local community?			
Role-play areas and read stories that reflect the diversity of children's experiences?			
Opportunities to make a display with the children, showing all the people who make up the community of the setting?			
Opportunities for people from a range of cultural backgrounds to talk about aspects of their lives or the things they do in their work?			

If you have ticked no to any question, use this as a basis to complete an action plan as on page 40 to identify what you need to find out more about and how to develop your practice or environment.

Understanding the World – People and Communities

THE UNIQUENESS OF YOUR CHILDREN – How much do you know about the children in your key group?

Do you know....	Yes	Where is the evidence?	No
Who moves eyes, then head, to follow moving objects?			
Who reacts with abrupt change when a face or object suddenly disappears from view?			
Who looks around a room with interest?			
Who smiles with pleasure at recognisable playthings?			
Repeats actions that have an effect e.g. shaking a rattle?			
Closely observes what animals, people and vehicles do?			
Who looks for dropped objects?			
Who becomes absorbed in combining objects, e.g. banging tow objects?			
Who knows things are used in different ways?			

POSITIVE RELATIONSHIPS – What do you do?

Do you....	Yes	When or where?	No
Encourage babies' movements through your interactions e.g. touching their fingers and toes and showing delight at their kicking and waving?			
Play hiding and finding games inside and outdoors?			
Plan varied arrangements of equipment and materials that can be used with babies in a variety of ways to maintain interest and provide challenges?			
Draw attention to things in different areas that stimulate interest, such as a patterned surface?			

ENABLING ENVIRONMENTS – Do you have?

Do you have.....	Yes	Where?	No
A range of everyday objects for babies to explore and investigate such as treasure baskets?			
Opportunities to provide novelty – make small changes in the predictable environment?			
Lift-the-flap books to show something hidden from view?			
A variety of interesting things for babies to see when they are looking around them, looking up at the ceiling or peering into a corner?			
Talk about photographs of babies' favourite places?			

If you have ticked no to any question, use this as a basis to complete an action plan as on page 40 to identify what you need to find out more about and how to develop your practice or environment.

Understanding the World – The World

THE UNIQUENESS OF YOUR CHILDREN – How much do you know about the children in your key group?

Do you know....	Yes	Where is the evidence?	No
Who explores objects by linking together different approaches: shaking, hitting, looking, feeling, tasting?			
Who remembers where objects belong?			
Who matches parts of objects that fit together, e.g. puts a lid on a teapot?			
Who enjoys playing with small-world models such as a farm?			
Who notices detailed features of objects in their environment?			

POSITIVE RELATIONSHIPS – What do you do?

Do you....	Yes	When or where?	No
Talk with children about their responses to sights, sounds and smells in the environment			
Talk about what the children like about playing outdoors?			
Encourage the children to explore puddles, trees and surfaces such as grass?			
Tell stories about places and journeys?			

ENABLING ENVIRONMENTS – Do you have?

Do you have.....	Yes	Where?	No
Opportunities outdoors for children to investigate features e.g.a mound, a path or a wall?			
A collection of sets of items for children to explore how objects can be combined together in heuristic play sessions?			
Opportunities in the outdoor area to investigate the natural world e.g. windmills and bubbles to investigate the effects of wind?			
Stories and information books about places, such as a zoo, to remind children of visits to real places?			

If you have ticked no to any question, use this as a basis to complete an action plan as on page 40 to identify what you need to find out more about and how to develop your practice or environment.

The EYFS: Am I getting it right? © Anita Soni & Sue Bristow

THE UNIQUENESS OF YOUR CHILDREN – How much do you know about the children in your key group?

Do you know....	Yes	Where is the evidence?	No
Who comments and asks questions about aspects of their familiar world?			
Who can take about some of things they have observed?			
Who talks about why things happen and how things work?			
Who is developing an understanding of growth, decay and changes over time?			
Who shows care for living things and the environment?			
Who looks closely at similarities, differences, patterns and change?			
Who talks about how environments might vary from one another?			

POSITIVE RELATIONSHIPS – What do you do?

Do you....	Yes	When or where?	No
Use parent's knowledge to extend children's experiences of the world?			
Support children with sensory impairment?			
Increase awareness of features of the environment in the setting and the immediate local area by talking to people, examining photographs and simple maps?			
Introduce vocabulary to enable children to talk about their observations and to ask questions?			
Help children to notice patterns?			
Examine change over time?			
Use appropriate words e.g. 'town' 'village'			
Encourage children to express opinions on natural and built environments using appropriate vocabulary e.g. busy, pollution?			
Pose carefully framed open ended questions?			

ENABLING ENVIRONMENTS – Do you have?

Do you have.....	Yes	Where?	No
Opportunities to explore the built and natural environment?			
Opportunities to observe things closely e.g. magnifiers			
Play maps and small world equipment for children to create their own environments?			
Opportunities to record findings by e.g. drawings			
Stories that help children to make sense of different environments?			
Stimuli and resources for children to create e.g. simple maps and plans, paintings, drawings			
Opportunities to design practical, attractive environments?			

If you have ticked no to any question, use this as a basis to complete an action plan as on page 40 to identify what you need to find out more about and how to develop your practice or environment.

Understanding the World – The World

THE UNIQUENESS OF YOUR CHILDREN – How much do you know about the children in your key group?

Do you know....	Yes	Where is the evidence?	No
Where in the environment or in which experiences does each child show a willingness to have a go?			
The activities and experiences that each child likes to find out about and explore?			

See Characteristics of Effective Learning – Playing and Exploring and Creating and Thinking Critically.

POSITIVE RELATIONSHIPS – What do you do?

Do you....	Yes	When or where?	No
Support the children without taking over or directing?			
Follow the child's lead in how they want to play?			
Model self-talk, describing what you are doing as you do it to show your thinking?			
Play with the children, encourage them to explore?			

See Characteristics of Effective Learning – Playing and Exploring and Creating and Thinking Critically.

ENABLING ENVIRONMENTS – Do you have?

Do you have.....	Yes	Where?	No
Reduced background noise so children can concentrate?			
First hand experiences at the appropriate level for the children?			
Uninterrupted time for the children to play and explore?			
Time, space, flexible resources, choice and control within warm key person relationships to allow children to develop rich play?			
Stimulating resources which are accessible and open-ended so they can be used in different ways?			

See Characteristics of Effective Learning – Playing and Exploring and Creating and Thinking Critically.

If you have ticked no to any question, use this as a basis to complete an action plan as on page 40 to identify what you need to find out more about and how to develop your practice or environment.

The EYFS: Am I getting it right? © Anita Soni & Sue Bristow

THE UNIQUENESS OF YOUR CHILDREN – How much do you know about the children in your key group?

Do you know....	Yes	Where is the evidence?	No
Who anticipates repeated sounds, sights and actions?			
Who shows an interest in toys with buttons and simple mechanisms and beginning to learn to operate them?			
Who seeks to acquire basic skills in turning on and operating some ICT equipment?			
Who operates mechanical toys e.g. pulls back a friction car?			

POSITIVE RELATIONSHIPS – What do you do?

Do you....	Yes	When or where?	No
Comment on the ways in which young children investigate how to push, pull, lift or press parts of toys and domestic equipment?			
Talk about the effect of children's actions, as they investigate what things can do?			
Support children in exploring the control technology of toys e.g. toy electronic keyboard?			
Talk about ICT apparatus, what it does, what they can do with it and how to use it safely?			

ENABLING ENVIRONMENTS – Do you have?

Do you have.....	Yes	Where?	No
Available robust resources with knobs, flaps, keys or shutters?			
Technology resources that children recognise into their play, such as cameras?			
Safe equipment to play with, such as torches, transistor radios or karaoke machines?			
Opportunities where children can use the machines like the photocopier to copy their own pictures?			

If you have ticked no to any question, use this as a basis to complete an action plan as on page 40 to identify what you need to find out more about and how to develop your practice or environment.

Understanding the World – Technology

THE UNIQUENESS OF YOUR CHILDREN – How much do you know about the children in your key group?

Do you know….	Yes	Where is the evidence?	No
Who can operate simple equipment e.g. turns on CD player and uses remote control?			
Who shows an interest in technological toys with knobs or pulleys or real objects such as cameras?			
Who shows skill in making toys work by pressing parts or lifting flaps to achieve effects such as sound, movements or new images each child has?			
Who knows that information can be retrieved from computers?			
Who can complete a simple program on a computer?			
Who can recognise that a range of technology is used in places such as homes and schools?			
Who can select and use technology for particular purposes?			

POSITIVE RELATIONSHIPS – What do you do?

Do you….	Yes	When or where?	No
Support and extend the skills children develop as they become familiar with simple equipment, such as twisting?			
Draw young children's attention to ICT apparatus?			
Encourage children to speculate on the reasons why things happen or how things work?			
Support children to coordinate actions to use technology, for example, call a telephone number?			
Teach and encourage children to click on different icons to cause things to happen in a computer program?			

ENABLING ENVIRONMENTS – Do you have?

Do you have…..	Yes	Where?	No
Opportunities for children to help press the button at the pelican crossing or speak into an intercom to tell somebody you have come back?			
A range of materials and objects to play with that work in different ways for different purposes for example egg whisk, torch, construction kits?			
A range of programmable toys, as well as equipment involving ICT, such as computers?			

If you have ticked no to any question, use this as a basis to complete an action plan as on page 40 to identify what you need to find out more about and how to develop your practice or environment.

THE UNIQUENESS OF YOUR CHILDREN – How much do you know about the children in your key group?

Do you know....	Yes	Where is the evidence?	No
Who explores and experiments with a range of media through sensory exploration, and using whole body?			
Who moves their whole bodies to sounds they enjoy, such as music or a regular beat?			
Who imitates and improvises actions they have observed e.g. clapping or waving?			
Who is beginning to move to music, listen to or join in rhymes or songs?			

See Physical Development and Understanding of the World – The World Birth to 11 months for further questions.

POSITIVE RELATIONSHIPS – What do you do?

Do you....	Yes	When or where?	No
Encourage babies to join in tapping and clapping along to simple rhythms?			
Notice the different ways babies move in response to sounds e.g. patting the floor when on their tummy?			
Encourage babies to make marks and to squeeze and feel media such as paint, gloop?			

See Physical Development and Understanding of the World – The World Birth to 11 months for further questions.

ENABLING ENVIRONMENTS – Do you have?

Do you have.....	Yes	Where?	No
A range of puppets that can guide along the table, or dance around on the end of a fist in time to some lively music?			
Big sheets of plastic or paper on the floor so that babies can be near or crawl on to it to make marks?			
Materials to encourage large motor movements e.g. sprinkling, throwing or spreading paint, glue, torn paper or other materials?			

See Physical Development and Understanding of the World – The World Birth to 11 months for further questions.

If you have ticked no to any question, use this as a basis to complete an action plan as on page 40 to identify what you need to find out more about and how to develop your practice or environment.

THE UNIQUENESS OF YOUR CHILDREN – How much do you know about the children in your key group?

Do you know....	Yes	Where is the evidence?	No
Who notices and is interested in the effects of making movements which leaves marks?			
The favourite songs each child joins in and sings?			
Who creates sounds by banging, shaking, tapping?			
Who shows and interest in the way musical instruments sound?			
Who experiments with blocks, colours and marks?			

POSITIVE RELATIONSHIPS – What do you do?

Do you....	Yes	When or where?	No
Listen with children to a variety of sounds, talking about favourite sounds, songs and music?			
Introduce children to language to describe sounds and rhythm e.g. loud and soft?			
Accept wholeheartedly young children's creations and help them to see them as something unique and valuable?			
Make notes detailing the processes involved in a child's creation, to share with parents?			
Help children to listen to music and watch dance when opportunities arise, encouraging them to focus on how sound and movement develop from feelings and ideas?			
Encourage and support the inventive ways in which children add, or mix media, or wallow in particular experience?			

ENABLING ENVIRONMENTS – Do you have?

Do you have.....	Yes	Where?	No
A sound line using a variety of objects strung safely, that will make different sounds such as plastic bottles filled with different things?			
A wide range of materials, resources and sensory experiences to enable children to explore colour, texture and space?			
Space and time for movement and dance both indoors and outdoors?			
Opportunities whereby children can experience live performances e.g. dancers and musicians from theatre groups?			
A wide range of musicians and story tellers from a variety of cultural backgrounds?			
Unusual or interesting materials and resources that inspire exploration such as raffia, textured wall coverings?			

If you have ticked no to any question, use this as a basis to complete an action plan as on page 40 to identify what you need to find out more about and how to develop your practice or environment.

THE UNIQUENESS OF YOUR CHILDREN – How much do you know about the children in your key group?			
Do you know....	Yes	*Where is the evidence?*	No
Who enjoys joining in with dancing and ring games?			
The familiar songs each child sings and the dances they know?			
Who is beginning to move rhythmically?			
Who imitates movement in response to music?			
Who can tap out simple repeated patterns?			
Who explores colour and sound and how they can be changed?			
Who understands that they can use lines to enclose a space, and then begin to use shapes to represent objects?			
Who is interested in and describes the texture of things?			
Who is beginning to construct, stacking blocks vertically and horizontally, making enclosures and creating spaces?			
Who joins construction pieces together to build and balance, with a purpose in mind?			
Who understands that different media can be combined to create new effects?			
Who manipulates materials to achieve a planned effect?			
Who uses simple tools and techniques competently and appropriately?			
Who can select appropriate resources and adapts work where necessary?			

POSITIVE RELATIONSHIPS – What do you do?			
Do you....	Yes	*When or where?*	No
Support children's responses to different textures?			
Introduce vocabulary to enable children to talk about their observations and experiences e.g. 'smooth' 'shiny'?			
Talk about children's growing interest in and use of colour?			
Support children in thinking about what they would like to make, the processes that may be involved and the materials and resources they might need?			
Talk to children about ways of finding out what they can do with different media and what happens when they put different things together such as sand, paint and sawdust?			
Encourage children to notice changes in properties of media as they are transformed through becoming wet, dry, and flaky and to think about cause and effect?			

ENABLING ENVIRONMENTS – Do you?			
Do you.....	Yes	*Where?*	No
Lead imaginative movement sessions?			
Provide a place where work in progress can be kept safely?			
Talk with children about where they see models and plans in the environment?			
Demonstrate and teach skills and techniques associated with the things children are doing?			
Introduce children to a wide range of music, painting and sculpture?			
Encourage children to take time to think about painting or sculpture that in unfamiliar to them before they talk about it or express an opinion?			
Provide resources for mixing colours, joining things together and combining materials?			
Have a holding bay where models and works can be retained?			
Plan imaginative, active experiences helping them to remember the actions of the story?			

If you have ticked no to any question, use this as a basis to complete an action plan as on page 40 to identify what you need to find out more about and how to develop your practice or environment.

Expressive Arts and Design – Exploring and using media and materials

THE UNIQUENESS OF YOUR CHILDREN – How much do you know about the children in your key group?

Do you know....	Yes	Where is the evidence?	No
How each child shows they are interested or want something?			
The sounds and noises or words each child uses?			
How each key child responds and reacts to interaction?			
How each child shows pleasure, fear and excitement?			
How each child gets other people to do things for him/her?			
How each child responds to new people or situations?			
How each child cues that s/he is ready to engage?			

See Communication and Language, Physical Development and Personal, Social and Emotional Development Birth to 20 months for further questions

POSITIVE RELATIONSHIPS – What do you do?

Do you....	Yes	When or where?	No
Follow the children's lead as they explore?			
Show you enjoy being with each child?			
Have a key person for each child who knows the child well and understands their needs and wants?			
Talk to children when you hold them or are with them to show they are secure and safe?			
Copy and turn take in conversations with each child?			
Make eye contact when talking to each child?			
Spend time being close with each key child?			

See Communication and Language, Physical Development and Personal, Social and Emotional Development Birth to 20 months for further questions

ENABLING ENVIRONMENTS – Do you have?

Do you have.....	Yes	Where?	No
Uninterrupted time to play and talk to the children?			
Individual time with each child when they are alert and happy to engage?			
Show and value the languages spoken by staff, children and parents?			
Opportunities for children to be near each other and 'chat'?			

See Communication and Language, Physical Development and Personal, Social and Emotional Development Birth to 20 months for further questions

If you have ticked no to any question, use this as a basis to complete an action plan as on page 40 to identify what you need to find out more about and how to develop your practice or environment.

THE UNIQUENESS OF YOUR CHILDREN – How much do you know about the children in your key group?

Do you know....	Yes	Where is the evidence?	No
Who expresses self through physical action and sound?			
Who pretends that one object represents another, especially when objects have characteristics in common?			
Who is beginning to use representation to communicate e.g. drawing a line and saying 'That's me'?			
Who is beginning to make–believe by pretending?			

POSITIVE RELATIONSHIPS – What do you do?

Do you....	Yes	When or where?	No
Show genuine interest and be willing to play along with a child who is beginning to pretend?			
Observe and encourage children's make-believe play in order to gain understanding of their interests?			
Sometimes speak quietly, slowly or gruffly for fun in pretend scenarios?			
Show interest in the children's creative processes and talk to them about what they mean to them?			

ENABLING ENVIRONMENTS – Do you have?

Do you have.....	Yes	Where?	No
A variety of familiar resources reflecting everyday life, such as magazines, telephones?			
Story boxes filled with interesting items to spark children's storytelling ideas?			
Additional resources reflecting interest such as cloaks and bags?			

If you have ticked no to any question, use this as a basis to complete an action plan as on page 40 to identify what you need to find out more about and how to develop your practice or environment.

Expressive Arts and Design – Being Imaginative

THE UNIQUENESS OF YOUR CHILDREN – How much do you know about the children in your key group?

Do you know....	Yes	Where is the evidence?	No
Who is developing preferences for forms of expression?			
Who uses movement to express feelings?			
Who creates movement in response to music?			
Who sings to self and makes up simple songs?			
The rhythms each child makes up?			
Who notices what adults do, imitating what is observed and then does it spontaneously when the adults are not there?			
Who engages in imaginative role-play based on own first hand experiences?			
Who builds stories around toys?			
Who uses available resources to create props to support role-play?			
Who captures experiences and responses with a range of media such as music, dance?			
Who creates simple representations of events, people and objects?			
Who initiates new combinations of movement and gesture in order to express and respond to feelings, ideas and experiences?			
Who chooses particular colours for a purpose?Who introduces a storyline or narrative into their play?			
Who plays alongside other children who engage in the same theme?			
Who plays cooperatively as part of a group to develop and act out a narrative?			

POSITIVE RELATIONSHIPS – What do you do?

Do you....	Yes	When or where?	No
Support children's excursions into imaginary worlds?			
Help children to gain confidence in their own way of representing ideas?			
Make the link between imaginative play and children's ability to handle narrative?			
Create imaginary worlds to describe e.g. monsters in stories?			
Help children to communicate through their bodies by encouraging expressive movement linked to their imaginative ideas?			
Introduce descriptive language?			

ENABLING ENVIRONMENTS – Do you have?

Do you have.....	Yes	Where?	No
Stories based on children's experiences?			
Opportunities to use story stimulus by suggesting an imaginary event or set of circumstances?			
Opportunities to extend children's experiences and expand their imagination through the provision of pictures, paintings, poems, music, dance and story?			
Opportunities to provide a stimulus for imagination by introducing atmospheric features in the role play area such as the sound of rain beating off the roof?			
Materials that are accessible so that children are able to imagine and develop their projects and ideas while fresh in their mind?			
Opportunities to use their skills and explore concepts and ideas through representations?			
Opportunities indoors and outdoors and support the different interest of the children?			

If you have ticked no to any question, use this as a basis to complete an action plan as on page 40 to identify what you need to find out more about and how to develop your practice or environment.

Expressive Arts and Design – Being Imaginative

The EYFS: Am I getting it right? © Anita Soni & Sue Bristow